OTHER BOOKS BY KIM KERRIGAN AND STEVEN WELLS

The Amazing Anthology of Writing, Grammar, and Vocabulary Tips: For People Short on Time—and Short on Patience!

Sound Advice for Successful Writing: Creating Powerful E-Mails and Letters in Today's Workplace

Punctuation and Language Usage Made Easy: Concise Grammar Guidelines for Busy Professionals

Words for the Wise: A Vocabulary Primer for the Precise Professional

Get a Grip on Business Writing: Critical Skills for Success in Today's Workplace

Published by Corporate Classrooms

~~~~~

Get a Grip on Supervisory Skills

Get a Grip on Finance and Accounting: Critical Skills for Success in Today's Business World

Get a Grip on Writing: Critical Skills for Success in Today's Business World

Get a Grip on Speaking and Listening: Vital Communication Skills for Today's Business World

Get a Grip on Grammar: Language Skills for Today's Business World

Published by Prentice Hall Direct, A Simon and Schuster Company

Making Civility Great Again

Making Civility Great Again

Improving Face to Face
Communication
in an Age of Chaos

Kim Kerrigan and Steven Wells

Published by Corporate Classrooms

Copyright © 2019 by Kim Kerrigan and Steven Wells

All rights reserved. No part of this book may be reproduced or transmitted in any form or by any means, electronic or mechanical, including photocopying, recording, or by any information storage and retrieval system without the written permission of the authors, except where permitted by law.

0402-19

Visit our website www.corporateclassrooms.com for more information about our company, workshops, and books.

ISBN 978-0972225014

Library of Congress Control Number: 2019938407

Dedication

We dedicate *Making Civility Great Again* to all Americans who remain civil in their daily encounters to create an even more empathetic and respectful country. Their efforts, whether small or large, help weave the fabric of America as a kind, compassionate, and peaceful nation.

As always, we are extremely grateful to our parents, Evelyn and James Kerrigan and Mary and Charles "Sam" Wells, for showing us the grace that civility bestows on those who choose to take the high road in life.

Acknowledgements

Once again, we extend our great thanks to Joseph M. Gaken for his superb assistance as we developed *Making Civility Great Again*. Joe's sharp observations and perceptive comments were much appreciated—and much needed—in the development of this book. Also, Joe's exemplary civility towards others continues to serve as a benchmark for us as we strive for greater civility in our own lives.

Table of Contents

Introduction to Making Civility Great Again i

Chapter 1 The Psychology of Civility 1

Chapter 2 Good Manners: The Soul of All Civility 31

Chapter 3 Genuine Listening: The Path to Understanding and Compromise 53

Chapter 4 Beware of Labels, Loaded Words, and Lax Listening Filters 67

Chapter 5 Know When and Why You Are Not Listening— and What You Can Do About It 87

Chapter 6 Connecting with People in a Positive, Productive, and Precise Way 103

Chapter 7 Your Oral Communication Speaks Volumes About Your Civility 123

Chapter 8 Empathy and Assertiveness: The Bookends of Civility 141

Chapter 9 Avoiding Roadblocks That Prevent Successful Communication 157

Chapter 10 The Top Ten Talking Turnoffs: The Quickest Way to Alienate Others 175

Chapter 11 Using the Tremendous Power of Nonverbal Communication 187

Chapter 12 Do Your Actions— and Expectations— Speak Louder Than Your Words? 207

Chapter 13 Managing Anger to Maintain Civility 227

Chapter 14 Frequently Asked Questions and Challenging Situations in Face to Face Communication 254

Chapter 15 The Mark of a Truly Civil Person 273

Introduction to Making Civility Great Again

We decided to write *Making Civility Great Again* to reduce the great discontent and divisiveness we have seen growing in America during the last few years. As anyone who has spent a lengthy amount of time in the United States can easily verify, the tone of our political, community, and personal relationships has grown to a shrill when controversial topics are discussed among people.

No longer does it appear we are a people who are eager to learn and mature in our thinking. We seem to hold fast to our old beliefs and seem to be fearful of any innovative ideas, concepts, and attitudes that conflict—and threaten—our existing ways of thinking and approaches to daily living. Equally disturbing, we seem unwilling to explore diverse ways of improving our towns and cities and strengthening the ties that initially bound us as families and communities (many of them filled with immigrants as well as first- and second-generation Americans), neighbors, classmates, team members, workplace colleagues, and, yes, even political allies and opponents.

It's clear to us the election of Donald Trump as president of the United States in 2016, when he defeated his opponent, Hillary Clinton, was a major turning point for the American people. In an historic way, we can measure the tenor of our national mood today as "BT" and "AT" ("Before Trump" and "After Trump"). But that is a far too simplistic analysis of the extreme discord that has been festering for years and is now at a fever pitch in America.

Let's not kid ourselves. The erosion of compromise and civility in our national life has been deepening for decades. It was probably inevitable we would reach this point now considering all the incredible changes we, as citizens of one of the leading and most highly revered countries in the world, have endured. Just look at the proliferation of recent technology (whether involving the Internet, cable television, cell phones, automobiles, and so forth) and the growth in millions of our immigrant population from places all over the world as two examples of change that have clearly altered the American landscape.

Then, consider the trauma and lingering wounds to our national soul caused by the events of 9/11/2001 when the Twin Towers fell in New York City and the planes crashed into the Pentagon and a field in Shanksville, PA. Think, too, about laws granting greater equality to women and the LGBTQ community; the rise of strident evangelicalism; and the ensuing, and seemingly endless, debate over the proliferation of guns in our country. Of course, there is the ongoing struggle (which, many times, appears endless) to secure the blessings of *full* civil rights for all Americans regardless of their color, sexual identity, or gender; and the continued fight to allow or ban abortion rights though the issue of abortion was legally settled by the United States Supreme Court in Roe vs Wade in 1973.

Certainly, we Americans, as a nation, have lost one of the vital characteristics that has, for over 200 years, defined us as a reasonable, kind, fair, and respectful people—civility. For generations, we have profoundly displayed civility in our daily interactions and communications with people who are both like us—*and unlike us.* We have traditionally shown such civility towards our leaders who work for the greatest good of their constituents and towards our laws enshrined in the Unites States Constitution.

Most of all, in the past we have demonstrated great civility in our national spirit because of our belief that all American citizens (whether born here or elsewhere) are entitled to dignity, respect, fairness, and, yes, a helping hand. This reverence for our fellow citizens only highlights the American notion that all of its men, women, and children should live each day with the security they will not want for food, healthcare, housing, and education—no matter what their income, educational background, sexual orientation or identity, culture, or race!

All of this naturally brings us back to how we manage our civil discourse. For starters, we need to stop shouting, blaming, and insulting others as well as using ethnic slurs or vulgarities to demean people. This requires us to be more articulate, calm, and humble when we speak to others. Equally important, we need to be much more focused, empathetic, and involved when we listen to other people.

It is also imperative we stop closing ourselves off to new (and often more effective) ideas for working together to resolve mutual problems. To this end, we need to think deeply—and creatively—about actions and activities that truly benefit the common good and not just a select number of people in the highest positions of our society.

One of the preeminent ways we can achieve these goals is to restore great civility to all of our daily interactions and communications, whether it be in our speaking, listening, or nonverbal behavior with others. Otherwise, we are destined never to reach compromise and contentment in our private, professional, or political discourse.

So, in pursuit of our objective to help you revive civility in all of your relationships, we created *Making Civility Great Again.* Our book provides you with the basic—and not so basic—information you need to enhance all of your communication with people you know and with strangers you meet. In this book, we initially show you how to be a more effective and attentive listener. We then give you many methods to use so you can be a more polished and proficient speaker. In addition, we point out the enormous power your nonverbal communication (aka body language) has on *all* the messages you receive and deliver during any discussion, argument, debate, or conversation you have with another person or a group of people.

Our book also examines the ways you can be more empathetic or assertive, depending on your particular situation, without being invasive or overbearing in both your personal and professional relationships. With this in mind, we reveal, throughout *Making Civility Great Again*, the *unproductive* ways you can inadvertently damage or destroy your communication with others. Then, we provide you with numerous (and, what we consider, realistic) solutions and guidelines to enrich your interactions with other people.

More to the point, our suggestions will assist you in avoiding, or, at best, minimizing uncomfortable communication situations. We also supply you with valuable tools to ensure you always remain even-tempered, reasonable, and respectful while you speak and listen to other people, no matter how difficult, insulting, or disrespectful they may be to you. As a result of reading this book, you are bound to sustain a much more productive dialogue with all people—even those who hold radically different views than you!

We are convinced, moreover, *Making Civility Great Again* will be your newest "go to" resource book whenever you want to project and promote civility with your family members, friends, colleagues, neighbors, or any other people with whom you wish to maintain a meaningful and memorable relationship. And we passionately believe by engaging in the types of communication we advocate in the book, you will make a tremendous contribution to the restoration of peace, honor, and civility in your life and in the life of all Americans!

~~~~~

Most of the communication methods we describe and encourage you to use in *Making Civility Great Again* derive from the communication skills training workshops we have given for over thirty years as co-owners of Corporate Classrooms. In this book, as in *Get a Grip on Speaking and Listening* (published by Prentice Hall Direct, a Simon & Schuster Company, in 1996), another book we coauthored, we share the communication techniques that have proven remarkably successful for our clients throughout the United States and Mexico.

We have presented our workshops to thousands of employees (including, CEOs, managers, directors, supervisors, and support staff) in a variety of companies and organizations, such as ATT, Marriott Corporation, New York Department of Transportation, Citrix Systems, AmeriCorps, Boston Public Library, Walt Disney Parks and Resorts, Chicago Youth Centers, Stop and Shop Supermarket Companies, Mount Sinai Medical Center, American Red Cross, KPMG Peat Marwick, Evangelical Lutheran Church in America, and Ricoh Systems. Furthermore, our close association with several nonprofit organizations have led us to present communication skills programs specifically designed for parents, families, and students associated with these institutions. So, people in a myriad of personal, professional, and community settings have successfully used the strategies put forward in *Making Civility Great Again* to enrich their communication and build greater rapport with those around them.

We wrote this book as a primer to guide people through both pleasant and particularly challenging communication situations to increase civility between people. It is our firm belief we can further our understanding and respect for others' viewpoints if we consciously engage in sound speaking and listening while we never lose sight of our self-respect, humility, and empathy.

We did not intend to develop *Making Civility Great Again* as a study with many footnotes and bibliographical sources (though we have listed a handful in this book). Nor did we set out to provide a book with a comprehensive list of data about people, events, and facts pertinent to recent changes in the political landscape of the United States of America.

We mainly aimed to share our reflections about the lack of civility in American life today. We have done so with numerous examples of people at all levels of society (including many in leadership positions) who demonstrate a sense of entitlement, indifference, and insensitivity in their daily behavior.

With these examples, we offer well-considered explanations for improving your level of courtesy so you can communicate with others with greater skill, patience, and respect. You will then be more confident and competent as you speak and listen to people with whom you interact in a personal, professional, or public setting.

A great deal of our communication expertise involves common-sense solutions. These solutions derive from an appreciation for individual differences, empathy for others' unique life situations, and a determination to conduct one's life in an authentic and open way.

The information in this book, consequently, will nourish you in several ways. It will make you more understanding of various cultures, more considerate of people's feelings, and more self-reflective about your own motives and goals. We are absolutely sure *Making Civility Great Again* will not only help you diplomatically navigate your way through the current divisiveness caused by political animosity or any other source of discontent; we are also confident this book will make you a much more civil and caring communicator in all of your personal and public interactions.

Ultimately, we aspired to make our book a wake-up call for all Americans to pull together once more—and not walk away from each other. If we truly walk the same path and attempt to communicate earnestly with all people, our great American democracy will continue to flourish with hope, healing, and harmony.

Chapter 1
The Psychology of Civility

Unlike Donald Trump, the 46th president of the US, whose campaign slogan was "Make America Great Again," *we never thought America wasn't great*! On the other hand, we did—and do—believe a strong decline in civility in recent years in America has led to many unintended consequences for our country and its citizens.

As we point out in different sections of *Making Civility Great Again,* this lack of civility, quite frankly, stems from an unhealthy focus on selfishness, greed, and power. Many Americans equate money with status, self-confidence with aggressiveness, and power with the freedom to do anything one pleases regardless of its ethics, legality, consideration for others, and long-lasting consequences.

In this book, we continually make the case that civility is the key to a healthy, happy, and harmonious nation. Therefore, we believe it is the duty of *every* American to promote civility in his or her daily interactions with people whether on American soil or foreign lands.

For example, an emphasis on civility requires us to be responsible and *responsive* to all those around us. This includes those who remain marginalized in America and are unable to share in many of the benefits our country offers to others.

A decent and equitable society would be concerned with protecting all of its citizens to be able to satisfy their most basic needs and have the opportunity to achieve their personal long-term goals. In such a society, these same people will have the chance to nourish their dreams while receiving respect for the contributions they make to our country.

A consciously civil society, with a collective conscience, would reach out to the hidden and, often invisible, Americans who are destined to live a life of misery—unless they receive a helping hand and greater access to the resources and riches from the country they love.

Specifically:

A civil society would reach out to people who need better housing.

A civil society would reach out to people who cannot afford healthcare.

A civil society would reach out to people who are hungry.

A civil society would reach out to people who depend on true justice as they move through the legal system whether at the municipal, state, or federal level.

A civil society would reach out to people who want, but can't afford, further education.

A civil society would reach out to men and women and allow them to make decisions about their own body.

A civil society would reach out to immigrants seeking asylum and make sure they and their families stay together.

A civil society would reach out to people who believe they have a right to worship—or not to worship—as they please.

A civil society would reach out to people who want to live their lives without interference, regardless of their preferred sexual identity and orientation.

A civil society would reach out to people who count on their news media to be fair, accurate, and substantial at all times.

A civil society would reach out to people who expect their president to be honest, dignified, loyal, empathetic, humble, just, responsible, and knowledgeable about America's history, laws, constitution, and relationships with other nations.

A civil society would reach out to people of all ages, races, and cultures who have a genuine desire to earn a meaningful living that helps them, and their families move toward a life of greater opportunities, comfort, freedom, and well-being.

~~~~

Most people would anticipate a fair amount of civility from those who mention their religion as one of the rocks in their moral foundation. Yet, many so-called religious men and women have been prominently fighting for a return to more conservative and traditional behavior patterns and simultaneously endorsing political candidates, parties, and policies that are hardly civil—if civil behavior is a nondenominational equivalent for applying the golden rule: Do unto others that you would do unto yourself.

The golden rule, regardless of being expressed as religious or secular behavior, definitely strengthens and reinforces positive behavior in a civil society. Because this tenet assumes a love of self, the principle of treating others as you would like to be treated seems an ideal way to help heal the current divisiveness and chaos in the United States of America.

Many pundits have noted the philosophy of the golden rule is being shamelessly distorted by one group, ultra-conservative evangelicals. This group has long been a motivational religious force in shifting American politics to a more conservative—and, some critics say, extremely repressive[1]—position in several areas of our government.

Nevertheless, the Evangelical movement has gained millions of adherents since the 1980s, especially in fighting what many refer to as the culture wars. Evangelicals have consistently been in the frontlines when controversial issues—like abortion rights, death penalty laws, gay and transgendered rights, home schooling, prayers allowed at public venues, and so forth—are debated on the national stage.

But, somehow, the golden rule, which is a basic principle of many major religions found throughout the world, has been conveniently disregarded by some evangelical groups during the last decade. Elsewhere in this book we talk about the superficiality of *symbolic* behavior and mention that people are more impressed by a person's actions and treatment of other people than by his or her words. In short, we stress how powerful it is to "practice

---

[1] Merritt, Jonathan, "Are Conservative Christians 'Religious Extremists'?" *The Atlantic*, March 10, 2016

what you preach." When you actually display your beliefs in your actions and reactions, people are far more apt to listen to you and imitate your positive behavior.

No matter how you apply it, the golden rule requires you to be actively involved with improving the lives of all people unrelated to their status and what they can personally do for you. This necessitates, of course, much humility, generosity, and courage on your part.

Further, those you help don't need your sympathy, pity, judgment, advice, or preaching. What they could use most is your genuine interest in helping them live *what they believe* will be a more productive, enriching, and satisfying life for themselves. If all of us in American society made a greater effort to be more giving in spirit and less judgmental in our policymaking and actions, we could solve many of our country's pressing problems in record time!

We can readily become more giving in spirit and less judgmental by not blaming others for the mistakes they have made during their lifetime. The past can never be recovered. So, we always must act on the premise we can't change the prior mistakes and poor judgement of anybody or any group—or what has happened as a result of these errors and unwise decisions. But we *can* change and improve our thinking and behavior as we move forward.

With this understanding, we can offer genuine forgiveness to those who have demonstrated less than exemplary behavior at various times in their life. It is clear understanding and forgiveness are the true hallmarks of a country whose goal it is to build a much more civilized and advanced society.

Exploring the Five Basic Psychological Needs[2]

One of the best and most practical ways to begin repairing the psychic damage in our society is reviewing the five basic psychological needs of all human beings. You can divide these five needs into the following categories: the need to know; the need to be recognized and affirmed; the need to feel secure; the need to belong; and the need to grow. After reviewing each of these needs, you will begin to realize an overwhelming majority of American citizens shares many of the same aspirations for a fulfilling life, including a cohesive family and community; a challenging and productive career; and a sense of honor, dignity, and compassion.

All of these needs are really the gateways to our common future and renewed strength as a civil society. We, as human beings, must remain aware these five basic needs motivate all of us in one way or another. By doing so, we will ensure reaching compromise on so many divisive issues.

Focusing on these five basic psychological needs during our private and public discussions could lessen the bitterness and contempt we have witnessed the last few years. Equally important, the reminder that all Americans are attempting to satisfy the same needs can be a prime motivator for working and living together, with much

---

[2] The material in the section "Exploring the Five Basic Psychological Needs" derive, in part, from Maslow's Hierarchy of Needs, a theory developed by American psychologist, Abraham Maslow, in 1943. Mr. Marlow further expanded on this theory in his book *Motivation and Personality* in 1954.

more understanding and civility, to create an even stronger and unified nation.

The Need to Know

You and your fellow citizens obviously don't want to remain uninformed about your community and government affairs. You want to know about matters, policies, and decisions involving you in relation to your local, state, and national government. This information may appear readily evident. Yet, many misunderstandings and problems (including angry confrontations and legal battles) occur at the community, state, and federal levels because of a lack of mutual knowledge between people.

On the other hand, when your eagerness to know about government and community-related issues is satisfied, you are more aware, and, therefore, more informed and comfortable. These results, too, are certain to make you a more informed citizen and a much better communicator.

You can easily satisfy your need to know by reading newspapers on a regular basis. In this way, you will be certain to keep abreast of local, state, and national news. Moreover, you should challenge and broaden your knowledge by reading in-depth news articles as well as the work of others with opposing points of view.

In the same way, you can make it a habit to watch various news programs on both cable and broadcast television with the goal of listening to people whose beliefs and opinions are unlike yours. This is sometimes difficult to do and can even be very disturbing when another person's viewpoints are radically different from your own. Nonetheless, you may find, by listening closely to such views, either a nugget of wisdom or an idea that can expand your outlook or alter your convictions.

The key to satisfying your need to know is deliberately attempting to be extremely knowledgeable in numerous areas. This endeavor will allow you to be an informed citizen and will ensure your worldview is based on facts, objectivity, and a strong awareness of events on all levels—community, state, national, and international.

We live in a highly technical environment in which we are bombarded with texts, emails, social media, radio, television, and the Internet. So, there is a great temptation to absorb only bits and pieces of the news from these sources. This, undoubtedly, can be dangerous for both you and those with whom you exchange information.

In a democratic society, it is urgent all citizens remain as aware as they can be of issues and events affecting them and their country. To do otherwise is clearly a breach of one's responsibility as a citizen. Each of us must always seek to know and understand our world and our part in it whether on a local, national, or global level. Only in this way can we be assured we are fulfilling our role as involved citizens.

The Need to Be Recognized and Affirmed

Like all people, you need—and want—to be recognized as an individual and affirmed as a human being. If every single person just took five minutes out of each day to be more civil to others, there would undoubtedly be a *substantial* decrease in misunderstandings, incorrect information, hurt feelings, and hostility in our country.

You can also adopt the daily habit of improving the quality of your civility by focusing on every person in your life as a distinct individual. In this age of ever-evolving and growing reliance on faster though impersonal communication, we often forget the significance of relating to people who have unique backgrounds, challenges, and abilities.

You can increase the comfort zone of your community immensely by making a point to develop a friendlier relationship with your neighbors, frequent your local stores more often, and take a greater interest in community groups that exist to help others or improve local conditions.

As an active listener, too, you can encourage new acquaintances to talk more about their families and individual experiences. Your thoughtful behavior will contribute to a community fabric woven with concern and respect. Your great interest in your fellow citizens as worthwhile human beings and their beliefs (religious, cultural, and otherwise) as valid and important will further affirm their individuality. Concurrently, your empathy towards other citizens will create bonds that inspire genuine civility within your own neighborhood and community.

The Need to Feel Secure

It is natural for all human beings to want to survive and prosper. So, it is essential our country builds a sense of security for everyone who lives here. Citizens who know they are safe and can satisfy their yearning for greater comfort and stability will experience less anxiety in their daily lives. Ultimately, these same people will be more productive, relaxed, and effective in their personal lives and in their roles as citizens.

It has become increasingly evident to numerous sociologists that a sense of security is of extreme importance to most citizens today.[3] Furthermore, in our current environment—dependent on speed, change, and, most of all, immunity from outside threats and violence—security has become even more significant and must be addressed on a more rapid basis.

People will also be more responsive to different ideas when others don't ignore their personal needs and situations requiring greater security. In addition, when peoples' hard work, honesty, and playing by the rules are rewarded, in financial or other ways, they are certain to feel more optimistic as both workers and citizens. This can only ensure our country moves along in a positive and healthy direction.

You and most Americans are quite likely to embrace change as a step to progress if, and only if, you honestly believe the quality of your life; contributions to your community and country; and dreams for your future are seriously considered by people with the power to ensure such change. This knowledge is especially relevant when our government enacts, alters, or rescinds any law, policy, or plan that directly affects its citizens and their loved ones.

It's important for you to consider that marginalized Americans experience fear in their lives every day. They fear the loss of the safety net which supports their right to live. Life without fear isn't part of a human being's basic

---

[3] Des Gasper (2005) Securing Humanity: Situating 'Human Security' as Concept and Discourse, Journal of Human Development, 6:2, 221-245

needs, but life without fear is part of his or her need *to feel secure.*

All marginalized people in the United States want to fulfill what for them are fundamental needs. Some of these fundamental needs are safe, habitable housing; enough food to feed everyone in their household; low-cost or no-cost healthcare options to maintain and nurture their physical and mental wellness; and viable forms of transportation to ensure travel to and from their workplaces and schools without much difficulty. Naturally, when they do satisfy these essential needs, they will be more productive in achieving an economically secure future. These marginalized people will then be adding to the growth of the American economy.

The Need to Belong

When you belong to a group, you strengthen your basic human need to socialize and share yourself with others. In doing so, you start to recognize more parts of your personality as unique because the members of the group identify and nurture your individual qualities and overall worth. These people, not surprisingly, often notice your personal skills and talents before you do!

Not only do you realize the value of human bonds when you are dependent on those around you to satisfy your various needs; you also develop an awareness of others' dependence on you to fulfill some of their needs. As a result of these connections, you demonstrate greater trust, responsibility, and optimism. You also become more understanding and empathetic concerning the needs and challenges of other people. While your needs for belonging are being met, you receive added benefits, such as an expanded sense of cooperation, self-confidence, and enthusiasm.

In this environment, you feel good about yourself and are not afraid to exhibit independent thoughts and actions. Being free to exercise your own judgment and ideas in relation to your contributions further gives you a stronger sense of self-sufficiency and personal pride. In time, you become less fearful of taking risks and seizing new opportunities.

In today's American workplace, this information has special relevance. For example, you and your coworkers will discover failing at something does not make a person a failure. You and your colleagues will also learn making a mistake is simply practice for doing something right later. In fact, several case studies conclude organizations actually lower costs when employees are free from the fear of making mistakes. Meanwhile, this research also proves employees increase their effectiveness and morale because their organizations display flexibility, tolerance, and understanding.[4]

Even in seemingly unimportant ways, you can do much to help others (not just work colleagues, but neighbors, friends, and others you encounter in your daily activities) feel they belong to a larger group or community. You can interact and socialize more often with people during your work and lunch breaks, daily walks, visits to your local libraries, shops, and gym, and before and after services at your place of worship. Additionally, you can organize community events, such as neighborhood block parties,

---

[4] Rieger, Tom, 2011 "How Fear Destroys Companies: Through Parochialism, Territorialism and Empire Building" April 20

yard sale events, bake sales, and holiday celebrations. Just make sure you *personally* invite everyone in your area to participate in the event!

The Need to Grow

All people want to improve and enrich their lives by having stimulating experiences. It's part of human nature to become restless when one feels bored or stagnant in the same position, locale, or situation. Therefore, you demonstrate greater kindness and empathy whenever you look for signs of apathy in others (especially young people) and present these people with new and perhaps more exciting learning opportunities, employment options, and recreational activities. This naturally takes much time on your part, but your efforts encourage more civil and motivated citizens—and a healthy and harmonious country!

With this type of involvement, you become a de facto leader in your community. Your leadership ability then has the power to influence many other individuals in your immediate locale.

So, it's necessary you see the many similarities between the roles of teacher and leader. It may also surprise you to learn outstanding leaders exhibit the same indispensable behavior that outstanding teachers display. For example, outstanding teachers and leaders stimulate people to respond clearly, accept challenges willingly, and utilize their skills fully while focusing on common goals.

You can adhere to some or all of the same guidelines followed by these forceful teachers and leaders in your daily interactions. Also, you can regularly appraise both your teaching and leadership ability to ensure you are communicating effectively with everyone for whom you are responsible.

By adapting easily to new and, sometimes, demanding situations, you demonstrate strength and calmness that will help others embrace change. You can also exhibit flexibility and openness to innovative ideas and ways of solving problems—and not feel threatened when others with less experience or authority introduce novel or different approaches to overcome a challenge.

So many problems remain stagnant and unchanging because we keep restating the problems using the very same words in the same way. If we were to explain a problem, simply in an opposite way (e.g. reverse the wording), we might find viable solutions to the problem more quickly and effectively—and with much less anxiety and anger.

Let's assume, for instance, you are part of a group of people who keep having a problem which you describe in this manner: "We keep receiving low ratings from our constituents whenever we send out surveys asking them what we need to improve. Yet, no matter what we do, our group can't seem to find a solution to improve the low ratings we receive in our surveys."

In the meantime, a fairly new intern in your organization suggests your group turn around the wording of the problem. She recommends stating it this way: "What do we need to improve so our constituents give us higher ratings?" Within a short time, you and your colleagues begin receiving much better ratings on the surveys you send to your constituents.

What causes this change in your group's results? Just maybe it has something to do with not only looking at old problems in new ways; it might also involve *rewording* all problems in new ways. This is a clever piece of wisdom all of us need to remember as we discuss individual or group problems and productive ways to resolve them.

Finally, as a competent leader, you can convey a genuine concern about the problems your friends and neighbors are facing and tactfully present strategies to help them improve their personal situations. To illustrate, you could offer to contact, on behalf of your friend or neighbor, a person in a very visible position in your community, state, or national government. Then, you could explain to this prominent person the specific challenges your friend or neighbor is currently confronting. Often, such access to people who have the power to change things can be an absolute lifesaver!

Also, you can, as a neighbor, friend, or community leader, encourage other people to participate in free (or low cost) community programs. You can, in addition, urge people to volunteer at a local facility that aids those who are homeless, hungry, or addicted to drugs or alcohol.

The Five Basic Psychological Needs Should Matter to All of Us

It's vitally important we start talking with—and listening to—people in *all* parts of America so we can establish common ground pertaining to the controversial issues facing us today. Unless we initiate communication of this sort, we will continue to witness more polarization between large groups of people throughout the United States.

It cannot be overstated that we Americans have many of the same desires and expectations: a dynamic family life; beneficial and affordable healthcare for our children and ourselves; educational opportunities that won't hurt us financially; well-constructed housing in safe, attractive, and affordable neighborhoods; a way of daily living that gives us a feeling of pride, accomplishment, and contentment; and belonging to a community that appreciates the contributions we make to our families, neighbors, and others. Considering all these factors, it is obvious people all over the United States have much on which they agree. And we need to keep emphasizing that observation!

So, why is there such opposition between people when discussing political topics? Before we answer that question, let's consider three factors that have a strong bearing on all people in the US regardless of their political leanings: anger, fear, and greed.

Anger, as we point out in Chapter 13 of this book, anger is a normal emotion, but it's always preceded by another feeling (or feelings). People in various regions of the United States of America are experiencing anger that might be attributed to a feeling of not being recognized for what they have contributed to the United States; a feeling of alienation from receiving the benefits of the newest technology sweeping across our country and the world; a feeling of helplessness confronting the violent crime and drug and alcohol addiction that prevails in so many parts of their communities; and a feeling of abandonment, despite being productive and hardworking citizens, by the very institutions they helped build over the years.

Fear is often one of the feelings preceding anger. But what types of fear currently exist among millions of Americans that are causing them both deep anxiety and discontentment? Certainly, there is a fear of change. Many, many people have assumed the America they knew when they were young would remain much the same country as they grew older.

They believed the familiar jobs and the education advantages in their area with which they were accustomed would be readily available to their children. Untold numbers of these now older Americans obviously took for granted their children would enjoy comparable benefits—in employment and education—their parents enjoyed years earlier. They also counted on their communities remaining occupied by people they had known for years. In a sense, the America they knew and with which they were content was an unbroken chain of sameness, regularity, and tradition.

These lifelong American citizens are now seeing new people of different ethnicities and colors—and with unfamiliar names and religions—moving into their towns and cities. These same citizens agonize over what has happened to the country they once knew so well.

So, along with their other fears, they are contending with the almost overwhelming fear of "the other," whether personified by one person or a group of people. For Americans conditioned to routine and conformity, "the other" represents a tremendous threat—a threat to their daily lives as they must deal with "strange" people who possess diverse habits, physical features, and values. They fear "the other" just because the person looks and acts in unusual ways.

Naturally, this fear leads to stereotypes, generalities, and irrational conclusions. In time, long-term (and, normally, rational) citizens of America greatly fear "the other" and begin viewing such an individual as potentially dangerous to their families and their way of life. Is it any wonder then "the other" becomes the target of angry Americans who blame this human being for being an intruder in their communities and for displaying uncommon behavior!

Then, there are the American citizens who fear modern technology and the latest business models will leave them behind. These citizens worry their traditional attitudes and skills won't have a place in this new economy. Of course, even greater fear permeates those who have limited education and workplace skills that could help them acquire additional wealth.

Every day, too, millions and millions of Americans fear their enormous lack of access to people in high positions or with abundant power. They know all too well that these influential people can—and often do—reward their family, friends, and colleagues with opportunities that ensure their financial future and active participation in the direction and growth of America. Meanwhile, those without connections linger in confusion, stagnation, and despair because they are devoid of connections to people who could possibly reduce their burdens or problems.

With fear so paralyzing and yet rampant today in America, we are all called upon to display the courage that stops and defeats the malignancy that fear represents. Fear destroys so much in our lives: hope, optimism, joy, creativity, adventure, and a closer bond with diverse groups of people.

Fear, on so many levels, eats away at our soul and destroys the essence of who we are and what we can be as both human beings and as Americans. In troubled times, like today, when groups of people exploit fear to frighten, intimidate, and pressure others in the United States, we need to say, "Enough is enough" because there isn't any good that comes out of fear for us and for our fellow citizens. Period!

As one of our most well-known and popular presidents in history, Franklin Delano Roosevelt (President 1933-1945) said during his first Inaugural speech in 1933: "The only thing we have to fear is fear itself." Though President Roosevelt's first Inauguration occurred in the midst of national devastation caused by the Great Depression in the United States, the wisdom of his words remains timeless and invaluable for all of us. Yes, Americans are facing new and significant challenges each day, especially in politics, but it is fear itself that remains our greatest barrier to civility.

Finally, many Americans, tragically, are both perpetrators and victims of the greed that underlies so much of the anger and discontent in every region of our country. On the one hand, many Americans, in their rush to live the "good life," perpetuate greed by purchasing things they don't really need or use. Much of what they buy is what they hope will be reflective of their status as well-off and, at the least, upwardly mobile people. So, they acquire video games played only occasionally; remodel kitchens in which cooking rarely takes place (because the homeowners are busy earning money to pay for a luxurious or up-to-date kitchen); or pay for a bigger and more expensive car than they actually need or can afford.

It is interesting—and sad—these Americans place an exceedingly high premium on money. They equate six-figure salaries or more, for example, with people of immense success. In the same way, they regard expensive gits as reflective of the gift giver's extreme generosity and sacrifice or the excessive cost of other objects (furniture, televisions, vacation trips, clothing, and so forth) as indicators of a person's growing wealth and success. No more do they pay much credence to the adage "It's the thought that counts."

These materialistic-driven Americans seem rarely, if ever, to consider their lives are far more comfortable than a countless number of their fellow citizens living in the midst of poverty. By thinking only seldomly (and superficially) about their life of ease, they don't fully realize how fortunate they are to have heat, running water, indoor plumbing, and other basic amenities that people lack in so many parts of the United States.

You might say such Americans have developed tunnel vision when considering their place in the American economy. It's apparent they are more concerned with the acquisition of things—and their economic status—than with the plight of others in both the rural and urban areas of America where poverty is rampant. Little do these strangers to deprivation know that, in fact, poverty is a constant condition in the lives of millions of people in the United States. [5]

---

[5] According to TalkPoverty.org, a project of the Center for American Progress, the 2017 overall poverty rate ($24,860 for a family of four) in the United States was 12.3% of the national population or 39.7 million people. And, also in 2017, the number of people living on a household income twice the poverty rate ($49,720 for a family of four) was 29.7% of the population of the US or 93.7 million people.

It's a moral outrage, in a country as wealthy as the United States of America, that anyone should suffer from malnutrition (though millions do); or cannot receive the most basic healthcare to maintain normal human growth; or is unprotected by proper hygiene when it comes to drinking water and bathroom facilities.

The people with tunnel vision mentioned earlier are either oblivious to the conditions facing millions of their fellow Americans—or they simply don't care that others suffer miserably each day while they "struggle" to maintain their place on the economic status ladder. Just maybe, by developing a *gratitude attitude* (which we define as an attitude reflecting much gratitude for the simple things one has in his or her life) these fairly prosperous Americans will understand all Americans are diminished whenever any fellow citizen is diminished in any way. We preach a great deal in the United States about unity and defending our American sisters and brothers in both good and challenging times. Yet, we often fall short of our ideals because of our anger, fear, or greed—or because of all three.

Fundamental to each of these emotions is the desire to protect oneself. So, it's natural for people to focus on their own needs and security first. Nevertheless, the equality of treatment, rights, and opportunities for all citizens is a basic truth in a democratic society. This, of course, requires every citizen to adopt an empathetic and compassionate attitude towards all other citizens so a spirit of fairness and solidarity will thrive within a democracy.

Reflecting on our own history, it is clear we, as a nation, are strongest when we work together for the common good. The citizens of the Unites States enthusiastically pulled together and showed incredible strength during some of our most disturbing and tragic national episodes: the Great Depression in the 1930s; the bombing of Pearl Harbor in 1941 and our participation in World War II; the assassination of President John F. Kennedy in 1963; and the terrorist attacks occurring in New York City, Washington, DC, and Shanksville, PA on September 11, 2001.

So, now, as we attempt to rebuild the broken parts of our country and revive our national spirit, we must again pay special attention to the extraordinary civility that made the United States of America one of the greatest societies in human history. This attention requires we recognize the five basic psychological needs that not only bind us together as human beings. It also demands we make these five psychological needs the cornerstone of any plan, policy, or law affecting all American citizens.

~~~~~

It is essential, in the meantime, that we focus on our mutual concerns in addressing problems affecting all of us. To this end, we must pay increased attention to the world around us and make a deliberate effort to observe changes in both our physical and human surroundings.

Many cities and towns have recently been promoting the "See Something, Say Something" campaign on posters, billboards, and other prominent places to encourage all people to be much more cognizant of their locale throughout the day and evening. People of all ages in America are being asked to notify appropriate officials about things that seem strangely different, potentially dangerous, or just odd in some way.

This is a very resourceful way to involve all citizens in a project that not only involves everyone; it is a movement that will have lasting benefits for everyone. With its emphasis on personal responsibility for the good of ourselves and our fellow citizens, the "See Something, Say Something" crusade highlights the importance of all people working *inclusively* to achieve a safer, more secure, and more harmonious society.

In the past, parents, teachers, and other adults told many of us to remain quiet if we didn't have a positive comment to make about another person or situation. These same authority figures also told us, especially when we were young and commented on a problem that was not our own, "Mind your own business because it's not your problem."

Using the same logic to the large areas of American life in need of improvement, we should not bother with any problem that doesn't *directly* affect us. This type of attitude in not only parochial; it's destructive because we cannot truly thrive as a nation while we allow conditions to exist that could harm our fellow citizens or prevent them from satisfying their basic human needs in any way. By remaining silent when you are aware of a problem—and the many risks it presents—you are complicit for its growth and the damage it does to others.

In other words, we, as American citizens, are not free if there are other Americans who are not free to pursue, as the Declaration of Independence reminds us, "life, liberty, and the pursuit of happiness." When all of us in America finally recognize that civil rights, women's rights, gay rights, students' rights, immigrants' rights, and rights for any marginalized group are actually *human rights*, then we will be a nation of *unified* citizens who honestly want only the best for others.

~~~~~

In all the debates and discussions about the current state of American society, there has been insufficient attention paid to the basic human needs of our citizens. Many of us take for granted the notion, because we are all part of the same nation, we understand each other's most pressing needs and desires. Obviously, the *assumptions* we have made about each other have resulted in many dire consequences in the last several years.

The divisiveness, disrespect, and anger in the United States of America goes far deeper than our particular alliance with a political party (or lack thereof), personal value system, or religious, racial, or cultural background. Outside forces, such as the extreme political upheaval following the 2016 Presidential Election, deeply alter and affect our observations and views. For example, we frequently experience much angst because we discover our strongly held political values are not shared by our family and friends.

Recognizing this disparity in our values with the people we thought we knew so well naturally leads to some psychological discomfort, including confusion, disbelief, and anger. It may even cause us to shut down emotionally and limit our communication with loved ones. This is especially evident when we believe our political differences are likely to lead to extremely vocal disagreements. By not feeling free to discuss our positions openly, we begin alienating ourselves from those closest to us. Our relationships with these people, unfortunately, then become more distant and unfulfilling—and, occasionally, unchanging.

So, we face two extremely critical questions. Do our deep-seated political beliefs truly help us to communicate with others for mutual understanding? Or are we afraid to espouse our views and convictions to others because we fear they will respond to us in a fierce or condescending verbal manner?

The answers to these questions alone should be the basis of some profound thinking when we search for the root causes of the communication breakdown and conflicts between so many people and groups in contemporary America. Clearly, it is time we honestly consider not merely *what* American citizens think, but WHY they think the way they do. This approach may be one way we can understand the damage done to the awareness, pride, confidence, sense of identity, and personal and professional progress of men and women in every region of the United States of America.

Older, white evangelicals became key players in Donald Trump's rise to power. However, many media accounts of Trump supporters lumped *all* evangelicals into the same group as intensely conservative, locked in a time warp of unrealistic expectations, and longing for an English-speaking white world. But, as in numerous situations when critics try to separate people neatly into distinct groups, the demographics aren't easily defined.

You've undoubtedly heard commentators and columnists talk about evangelicals who have fervently backed

Donald Trump. However, the facts in an article, "This Diverse Group of Evangelicals Is Trying to Take Back the Faith,"[6] (published in the Huffington Post on October 5, 2018) provides a unique perspective. The article, written by Carol Kuruvilla, points to another group of evangelicals who recently (September 2018) met during a conference called The Chicago Invitation. First of all, Ms Kuruvilla makes it clear this group aims to "reclaim a faith tradition" from the older, white, and, usually, male members of the Evangelical movement who have sought to promote a blindly loyal following for Donald Trump and the Republican Party.

In reality, according to a 2017 study by Public Religion Research Institute,[7] thirty-five percent of evangelicals identify as black, Latino, mixed race, or other. The younger generation of evangelicals (under thirty) claim a white membership of only fifty percent. The average age of evangelicals, moreover, has been dropping for years.

Older, white evangelicals, more often than not, fear the changing racial makeup of the United States, based on an article published in Religion News Service in July 2018. This article indicates fifty-two percent of older, white express apprehensiveness about nonwhite people becoming the majority of the population by 2043. This apprehension reflects many older, white evangelicals' pessimistic attitude about immigration: extreme distrust of non-Christian religious views, strict opposition to open borders, and irrational fear of all refugees as dangerous or unhealthy.

---

[6] Carol Kuruvilla "This Diverse Group of Evangelicals Is Trying to Take Back the Faith" *Huffington Post* October 5, 2018

[7] Cox, Daniel PhD, Jones, Robert P. PhD 2017 "America's Changing Religious Identity" Public Religion Research Institute (PRRI)

On the other hand, all other religious groups within the evangelical movement, including a majority of younger (under thirty) evangelicals, hold positive opinions of the changing racial makeup of the country.

Furthermore, younger and nonwhite evangelicals have adopted a new commitment to "love and protect all people—including indigenous people, immigrants and refugees, LGBTQ[8] people, people with disabilities, and the poor. The leaders pledged to care for the Earth, resist white nationalism, defend the dignity of women, and embrace America's growing racial and ethnic diversity."[9]

Here again are more of the PRRI observations: Older, white evangelicals still fight the culture wars of decades past while younger adult evangelicals embrace the new cultural norms. In fact, nearly eighty percent of younger evangelicals and people of color in the Evangelical movement support same-sex marriage, and over sixty percent agree abortion should be legal and readily available for all women.

Likewise, while Donald Trump's opposition to immigration reverberates with older, white evangelicals, younger adult evangelicals increasingly support the Deferred Action for Childhood Arrivals program and a definite path to citizenship for all immigrants. In addition, older white evangelicals' excuse Trump's alleged indiscretions, divisive speech, and misshapen policy priorities. This, of course, alienates younger members of the

---

[8] LGBTQ: Lesbian, Gay, Bisexual, Transgendered, and Queer

[9] See 5.

Evangelical movement and moves them toward a more progressive and tolerant position.

Evangelicals comprise about one-fourth of America's current population. This group increasingly splits between a conservative, Trump-aligned block, and a more liberal block devoted to more progressive causes, such as immigration and acceptance of other cultures. The growing divide within evangelical Christianity isn't new, but it appears to be widening under Donald Trump's tenure.[10]

So, you will see references to evangelicals who support Donald Trump and his policies in parts of *Making Civility Great Again*. These evangelicals are, more often than not, older and white American citizens. More important, when you read about filters and labels in various chapters, remember what you've read here.

It is inaccurate—and dangerous—to divide groups of human beings, such as evangelical Christians, into broad and ambiguous categories for the sake of mere convenience. It's vitally important for you to dig deeply and think critically before you make sweeping assumptions about the attitudes, beliefs, and behavior of evangelicals or any other group. This self-reflection and thorough analysis not only encourage your objectivity when observing current events; it also makes you a more thoughtful and precise communicator.

One of the great ironies of the Evangelical movement is that many of its older and white leaders dismiss people who don't agree with their beliefs or attitudes. Though

---

[10] Bacon, Perry Jr, Thomas-DeVeaux, Amelia 2018 "How Trump and Race Are Splitting Evangelicals" FiveThirtyEight (an acquisition of ABC and affiliated with Nate Silverman)

these same evangelicals frequently mention inclusiveness, they appear to use this concept selectively. For example, a number of these evangelicals cannot accept those who don't believe in God; those who have abortions; those who are gay; those who are transgendered; or those who, in any form, contradict the Evangelical movement's sense of morality. They have also shown a steadfast desire to include prayers in public schools and during public events despite a large outcry from other citizens.

The same group sought to support and defend a man whose personal characteristics its members formerly regarded as reprehensible in any moral person, let alone a presidential candidate. One can easily conclude these strident evangelical Christians primarily supported this candidate—Donald Trump—to strengthen their opposition for granting basic civil rights to millions of Americans who they perceive are different from them or with whom they disagree.

When evangelicals do extend forgiveness to a person (such as the president of the USA) for specific transgressions, the forgiveness seems to be given with the subtle expectation of something in return from that person. The same spirit, on the contrary, seems not to apply to all others who have stumbled or behaved in an equivalent way if they have nothing to offer the evangelicals in return.

It appears, too, people who possess a particular moralistic streak have considerable difficulty accepting a person for whom and what he or she is. Genuine acceptance of a person is respecting his or her values, ethics, and unique approach to living an authentic life. To put it another way, people who truly accept others do not try to change them.

Chapter 2
Good Manners:
The Soul of All Civility

Today, millions of people in American society bemoan the glaring lack of courtesy and consideration in both private and public settings. So, one often hears a variation of the following question: Where have all our manners gone? Though there are still untold people who believe in—and display—courteous behavior, it is obvious a lack of concern for others by so many of our citizens has hurt us as a nation. It is also depressing to note the more self-centered we behave, the more we minimize our civic responsibility toward our fellow Americans.

Look carefully around you and you will observe the disappearance of simple courtesy by people you encounter in person or on television and radio or via other electronic communication. Rude, vulgar, and discourteous conversation has replaced what once was politeness characterized by discussions of distinct ideas in a calm and friendly manner. Naturally, our family, friends, professional colleagues, public figures, and media personalities all play a major part in defining the quality of communication in modern America.

Night after night we watch cable news and listen to the latest criminal charges against different people, outrageous scandals, and devious political maneuvers. The playbook seems full, yet another appalling chapter appears. Coarse language has become commonplace in our public discourse. Unfortunately, it doesn't even surprise us anymore.

Frequently, a number of media personalities set the communication channels ablaze with new terminology, such as *alternative facts*[11], *fake news*[12], *chain migration*[13], and *stable genius*[14]. These words all but destroy any civil and sensible communication between formerly principled and well-mannered people.

Across the globe, too, Americans have acquired a reputation for arrogance, bad manners, and lack of sophistication and refinement. The American image in many parts of the world, sadly, has become one of brashness, bravado, and boorish behavior.

---

[11] *Alternative facts* U.S. Counselor to the President Kellyanne Conway coined the phrase during a *Meet the Press* interview on January 22, 2017. She attempted to defend White House Press Secretary Sean Spicer's statement about the number of people attending Donald Trump's Presidential inauguration . The interviewer, Chuck Todd, asked Ms. Conway to explain Spicer's attempt to "utter a provable falsehood." Conway's response suggested Spicer was discussing "alternative facts". Todd replied, "Look, alternative facts are not facts. They're falsehoods."

[12] *Fake news* is false or misleading information distributed to discredit a person, place, or event. It often is distributed by online social media, but fake news has appeared in some mainstream media outlets.

[13] *Chain migration* (or "family reunification") authorizes legal US residents or green card holders to underwrite a legal immigration process for a family member. It is the most common legal form of immigration to the United States.

[14] *Stable genius* became a term Donald J. Trump used to boast about his vast knowledge potential and his mental stability. Alexandra Petri wrote about President Trump's *stable genius* in a column in the *Washington Post* on January 12, 2018.

It's equally evident people in the United States have received harsh criticism from other citizens for disregarding demands for greater civility and higher standards of conduct. On a much wider scale, the United States of America has demonstrated national incivility by involving itself in very costly and futile conflicts under the guise of establishing more stable and democratic governments in many other countries. For example, we have placed ourselves in several precarious situations and damaged our reputation in the world by dictating what other countries *should* do to be more like us. Additionally, our nation has used its vast military capacity and global power to force its way of life and government standards on nascent democracies and long-standing cultures (with lifestyles, values, and traditions much *unlike* ours), who have not even requested our assistance!

Still, we Americans can be—and should be—proud of what we have accomplished in various parts of the world with civil, respectful, and poised discourse. We should not let people who flagrantly display incivility in speech, manner, and dress harm our reputation, in any way, either in the United States or abroad. On the contrary, all American citizens must again practice the courtesy, empathy, and sound judgement that made our country not only a leader, but a model, for decades for people all over the globe.

~~~~~

In our society, there is a great deal of informality in our interactions with people we know well; with people who are mere acquaintances; and with people who are complete strangers to us. The rituals involved in our socializing, business practices, schooling, and community life (to name a handful of activities) have become so informal in many parts of our country that it's hard to remember formality was once an enormous, important, and *expected* part of our civil life.

For example, people, not too many years ago, were concerned about their use of proper language on a public street. They were also concerned about whether they were well-dressed for a wake (visitation) or funeral, wedding ceremony, or a dinner at a friend's home. Even while using a public mode of transportation, such as flying on a commercial flight or riding in a passenger train, they wanted to present themselves in a more formal, or at least, a more fashionable way than usual.

Today, however, you see men and women attend a wake or visitation, or even a funeral, in a pair of shorts and sandals or wear sweat pants and a jersey (sometimes emblazoned on the front with what some may consider offensive language). No longer are we shocked to hear adults, while driving their automobiles, scream obscenities at other drivers nor to see people staggering and shouting, while inebriated, on a crowded subway train.

Most of us don't even expect another person to hold a door for us anymore as we both enter a store at the same time. Nor do we expect to hear the graciousness associated with the words "please," "thank you," "I'm sorry," "pardon me," "excuse me," or "you're welcome" when we are in department stores, fast food restaurants, city or state offices, coffee shops, museums, fine dining establishments, or drug stores. It's as if we have become immune to good manners and good taste.

Equally discouraging is the ubiquitous response "no problem" commonly used by people when responding to others who have conveyed an expression of etiquette. Just hearing the words "no problem" one is left to wonder to what extent has a minor courtesy become a problem!

How did we reach this point? Millions of Americans lament "the way things used to be." They are constantly confused and angered by the absence of manners (aka an absence of civility) exhibited by people today in both private and public settings. With good reason, they wonder if this lapse in civility is indicative of a steep decline in our morals; a lack of respect for other human beings; an unwillingness to be generous to people beyond our immediate social circle; a lessening of our self-respect; or a preoccupation with our own needs and more.

It's a combination of all these factors and more. But it's also a lowering of our expectations in being the best, most honorable, and generous people we can—and should—be if we are to reap the benefits of a truly civil society. We will have become an exemplary nation once again when civility is foremost in the mind and behavior of every American citizen.

In whatever direction one looks, there is evidence of the low expectations and inconsiderate behavior by our fellow citizens: tossing litter on the ground; urinating in public; playing loud music in cars (that not only invades others' comfort zone; it causes their vehicles to vibrate); leaving their table in a self-service restaurant full of food crumbs and containers half-full of liquid; parking a car or truck beyond established boundaries (and, thus, preventing another person to park their vehicle easily); being oblivious to holding up a line of traffic because of texting or using a cell phone inappropriately (and, often, illegally); talking and laughing so loudly in a restaurant that it interferes with the quiet conversations and thoughts of other patrons; using vulgar language at sporting events that many parents don't want their children to hear; acting belligerently (or even violently) because their parking space has been taken after they shoveled snow off the space; chatting frequently during a film or play at a theater; cutting people off while driving in traffic; permitting toddlers and young children to run around wildly in a restaurant or another public setting without thinking how their playing may bother people nearby; threatening teachers and administrators because of disagreements over a policy affecting their children; failing to report the lack of soap and toilet tissue in a public restroom (and, thereby, inconveniencing people who later wish to use the same facility and avoid contracting germs); refusing to acknowledge the extra effort made by others on one's behalf; allowing infants to cry continually in a restaurant or other establishment (and never making an effort to remove the infants away from other patrons); and crossing a street when an electronic sign clearly indicates "Don't Walk" because they are talking on their cell phone or just simply being inconsiderate to drivers of motor vehicles. And the list goes on and on and on as we see more proof of the low expectations and thoughtless behavior of American citizens.

~~~~~

In 1989, Stephen Covey wrote *The 7 Habits of Highly Effective People*. In his book, Mr. Covey introduced the idea that we all have emotional bank accounts.

> "An Emotional Bank Account is a metaphor that describes the amount of trust that's been built up in a relationship. It's the feeling of safeness you have with another human being."
>
> —Stephen Covey

Now, in a comparable way, people need to pay attention to their civility accounts. In reviewing the current atmosphere of American society, it's clear many people—including friends, family members, and strangers—must be extremely overdrawn on their *civility bank accounts*. Some of these people realize they are dangerously close to a zero balance: void of empathy, understanding, and compassion in their account. Yet, they continue to use their remaining balance in ways that demean, discredit, and disenfranchise their fellow Americans. In other words, these "civility over spenders" are clearly bankrupt of civility.

What is the economic price we pay for the incivility of millions of our citizens? Obviously, people whose psychological well-being is shaken or shattered by the uncivil behaviors of others will seek comfort or reassurance in their many visits to doctors or therapists. Others, because of high anxiety caused by the threatening and destructive conduct of those around them, may find solace in overconsumption of alcohol or drugs or engage in reckless activities. Often, these people end up in hospitals or rehabilitation facilities for both severe physical and psychological problems.

So, while you and your friends may—along with knowledgeable United States economists—bemoan the massive financial deficit facing our country today, you may want to consider what our country spends annually in dollars and cents all because of the negative effects caused by incivility. In the workplace alone, incivility costs the United States of America millions of dollars each year.

The research and polling company Gallup released a study called *State of the American Workforce* in 2013.[15] This particular study (with data collected from 2010 through 2011) showed unhappy workers in the United States costs American businesses almost $550 billion each year in lost productivity.

The study defined people who don't care about their company and will not exert themselves to help it grow as unhappy or disengaged workers. Could it be any more apparent that a lack of civility throughout contemporary America not only hurts and traumatizes its citizens; it also costs our country millions of dollars to repair the damage done when people treat those around them in rude, abrasive, and counterproductive ways? As with any financial bankruptcy, the results for civility bankrupt individuals can be both startling and long-lasting: a poor civility record, difficulty receiving additional help from other civility sources, and a tremendous inability to reestablish their good credit as people with a healthy civility.

Similarly, America seems very unaware of its huge civility deficit towards its own people and its neighbors throughout the world. The same people who make daily pronouncements about the enormous economic problems plaguing the United States government are amazingly clueless about the harm inflicted on our country by millions of citizens with their blatant disregard for civility and

---

[15]. "State of the American Workplace: Employee Engagements for US Business Leaders" Gallup, Inc. 2013

its effects on others. All of the pent-up anger, reflected in the frustration, insults, and disrespect of these people in the USA is a strong indication we, as a *nation*, are on the verge of becoming bankrupt when it comes to civility.

People often say you can tell a lot about the quality and moral fiber of a country in its treatment of its most helpless, hopeless, and marginalized citizens. Well, as we review the past few decades in the US, one could argue our activities (as citizens, voters, neighbors, political observers, and so forth.) have created an emotional vacuum that not only has shocked multitudes of people on all four corners of the earth; it has lowered our standing in the world as a nation of people whose *first* priority for much of its history has been the promotion of the common good.

From the time we are young, most of us in American society learn the importance of politeness from our parents and other close relatives and friends who care for us. We learn to say "thank you" to anyone who extends a courtesy to us whether someone is holding a door for us; placing a meal in front of us; helping us put on our coat; bagging our groceries at the supermarket; confirming an appointment for us on behalf of a doctor or dentist; giving us a hand when we have fallen; or any of the thousands of other gestures people offer to assist us and show compassion for whatever task or undertaking we are facing at the moment.

In addition, we are taught to apologize to others, and to say "I'm sorry" or "Excuse me" for causing them any inconvenience, delay, or slight; for being rude or abrasive to them; or for making them feel uncomfortable or disrespected. We also remember to preface all of our requests with the word "please." Our parents and other care providers instruct us to say "please" so we don't appear demanding, selfish, or superior in our words and actions as we interact with others, no matter if we are 3, 8, or 20 years old. Up to now, such lessons in civility have stayed with us through our lifetime and have helped us socialize amicably with many different individuals.

~~~~~

Civility, moreover, has everything to do with building a community among people. That's why little acts of courtesy and graciousness, such as our frequent use of the words "please" and "thank you," create an even greater sense of community for us wherever we are located. Derivatives of the word *civility* loom all around us to reinforce the idea that courtesy, politeness, and good manners are the essence of any civilized society that honors the dignity and uniqueness of every human being. So, it's not surprising to see the word *civil* used extensively in our daily life: civil marriage, civil rights, civil trial, civil liberties, civil servant, and so forth.

All of these designations relate to strengthening a respect for our leaders, laws, public property, customs, rights, and behavior. It naturally follows that discourse in our community life (which, of course, is in the public sphere) adhere to the same standards we maintain in all of our other civil conduct. When we communicate with people anywhere, we must do so with profound respect for their boundaries; a reverence for the harmony of our community life; and the maintenance of the common good as prescribed in so many of our public documents, laws, and proclamations. Yet, as many people grow older, they seem to forget—or they find them unnecessary—the basic lessons of civility they acquired earlier in their life.

James O. Wilson and George Kelling wrote an article, "Broken Windows: Police and Neighborhood Safety," that was first published in *The Atlantic Monthly* in 1982. This article became the basis for the Broken Windows theory which, in turn, was the foundation for the way people in law enforcement approached wrongdoing and crime several years ago. The focus on broken windows by Mr. Wilson and Mr. Kelling was fundamentally a metaphor for dealing with crime and disorder in city neighborhoods.

The concept was put into practice and was widely used by Police Commissioner William Bratton in New York City in the 1990s. Essentially, advocates for this type of reform earnestly believed fixing small problems in neighborhoods—like broken windows—would prevent the creation of larger problems that lead to greater urban decay, turmoil, fear, and violence. As a result, the theory and its implementation received extensive news coverage.

In a way, the "Broken Windows" metaphor relates to the development of greater civility within a neighborhood. This, of course, affects our cities, states, and nation in a positive way. For example, little courtesies, such as the exchange of polite and heartfelt comments ("Please," "Thank you," "I'm sorry," and so forth) would, no doubt, lead to more empathetic and compassionate behaviors in the world at large.

In our effort to recapture the civility and integrity that once were parts of the American spirit, it is clear we need to start with the basics of social propriety and then keep expanding our focus on the innumerable situations in our daily life that demand more civil behavior. Only in this way can we turn the direction of a pervasive greed and self-centeredness found in every region of our country into a healthier direction. This new direction, with its emphasis on greater civility, will truly head us toward a climate of cooperation, respect, and caring that thrives in the collective heart of every productive, successful, and lasting society.

What is even more amazing about applying the "Broken Window" theory to a restoration of American civility is that it involves *everyone* in this country and does not cost the government or any individual to expend *any* money, taxes, or financial contribution of any kind. It only requires a commitment from each of us who wants a more supportive, understanding, and connected citizenry. This commitment simply asks us to adapt our daily behavior and communication so both are *always* consciously employed for the betterment of all the people living in our country. In this way, we can, once again, celebrate the common good of the USA.

~~~~

While considering topics to cover in this book, we debated whether to include a section on the effects of *instant gratification* on civility in the public sphere. We finally decided to address this subject because we spend so much of our daily life satisfying our own needs, wants, and desires.

It appears we spend a great deal of our precious time requesting information; ordering food or drinks; purchasing products; checking in with various government agencies regarding our benefits (tax returns, food stamps, social security and disability checks, Medicare coverage, and so many others); resolving a financial problem with our bank or credit card company; and standing in line at a department store, grocery store, ticket agency, and city office to obtain both tangible and intangible materials that our patience has diminished substantially while our annoyance and anger have increased proportionally in these situations.

Not surprisingly, this behavior has been a major force in reducing our ability to remain civil when we are feeling pressured by time; ignored by others; and angry with the poor and inconsistent customer service exhibited in commercial, retail, and government settings throughout our country today.

Over the last several years, different professionals in the academic and business world have studied the instant gratification rates of Americans in various circumstances. It is hardly shocking to learn the rate of patience in people, particularly those whose lives are heavily reliant on technology (computer programs, smart phone apps, text messages, and so forth), has been declining steadily and rapidly during this period.

People often receive faster service when purchasing products and services online: downloading music and films; arranging transportation to and from an airport; arranging potential dates; requesting the latest news; and, in general, acquiring what they perceive as extremely important personal information within minutes, if not seconds. Ankit Oberoi, writing for *Website Magazine*, estimates forty-seven percent of visitors will leave a website if the initial page takes over two seconds to load. Another forty percent will leave a website if the initial page takes more than three seconds to load.[16]

Consequently, people have cultivated their own sense of instant gratification for every part of their personal and professional life. Of course, their need for instant gratification has drastically lowered their level of civility and skills in developing a warm rapport with both the people they know well and those they hardly know at all.

~~~~~

One of the most bothersome examples of instant gratification has to be the inappropriate and impractical use of cell phones. It is also one of the *most invasive* interruptions of our privacy. No matter where you are, what time of day it is, or the setting in which you find yourself, wait long enough (not hours, but minutes, and, very often, seconds), and a person with a cell phone will likely invade your personal space. As soon as the cell phone user arrives, your serenity, your quiet, and your peace of mind all leave quickly!

Though the ubiquitous use of cell phones by millions of Americans didn't occur until the late 1990s, cell phones have come a standard feature of most environments in which people gather. And, for some odd and unexplained reason, cell phone decorum has taken on a life of its own.

People certainly don't apply the traditional rules of etiquette, found in so many parts of our daily lives, to their cell phone usage. On the contrary, millions of people seem to follow the "anything goes" rule of etiquette while they utilize their cell phones. The people who employ

---

[16] Oberoi, Ankit "5 Reasons Visitors Leave Your Website," *Website Magazine,* March 20, 2018

their phones like this either don't care or are oblivious to the fact their cell phone conversations might be—and probably are—disturbing someone who is reading, writing, studying, or simply reflecting about things in his or her mind.

Let's be very clear about this behavior! Unbecoming cell phone usage is not discriminatory. Everyone—children, middle-aged adults, and seniors are all part of the cell phone craze. Many of these people seem to have no problem using their cellphones in situations that impair the quality of life for their fellow citizens. There are uncountable people, for instance, who prefer to be alone with their thoughts or read (and unhampered by a cell phone conversation) even in busy surroundings full of people, such as restaurants, public parks, beaches, bookstores, and movie theaters.

But we are not just complaining only! We also are offering a solution for improving the lack of civility in our daily communication exchanges. The next time the phone companies try to sell you on a new cell phone plan, ask them if they offer an NIP plan: Noninvasive Privacy Plan whereby your cell phone keeps you alert to your cell phone etiquette (or lack thereof) by shutting off your phone anytime you are talking on it within four feet of another human being! What do you say? Why not join the millions of Americans who are now demanding they want more privacy and quiet in their lives?

~~~~~

Few people in today's world would deny the tremendous value and numerous benefits of modern technology. Most people will acknowledge that technology products in the last decade alone have made the workings of our daily lives immensely easier, faster, and more comfortable.

But all of these benefits have come at a steep price for people who also wish to have a more harmonious and civil society. For example, some people become very annoyed when delayed, or otherwise inconvenienced, by the slow movements of an elderly person.

Picture this situation:

An eighty-seven-year-old woman is purchasing her groceries at a typical grocery store in an urban area. The twenty-something cashier (who has a very matter-of-fact, detached, and perfunctory manner) tells the woman in a demanding tone of voice that the total of her bill is $25.74.

Upon hearing that amount from the cashier, the customer then begins searching for money in her pocketbook because she wants to pay with cash. As the lady searches for her money, it is obvious to the customers behind her as well as to the cashier that the customer's movements are quite shaky and tentative.

After a few seconds, the customer pulls out a twenty-dollar bill and says, "I do have a five-dollar bill, too, but I want to save it for later. But I know I have other dollar bills and the required change somewhere in my purse."

She starts looking in her pocketbook again and locates four one-dollar bills. Then she places the dollar bills on the counter as she continues to mutter, "I'm sure I have 74 cents in change." Finally, after a whole minute has passed, she retrieves two quarters, two dimes, and four pennies. With a big smile, the lady hands the change to the cashier who remains impassive.

At this point, two of the four middle-aged customers who were behind this customer in the line, leave without a word to stand in a shorter line. The two remaining customers, though they have rolled their eyes several times and quietly mentioned to each other how slow old people are, have remained in the line and waited for the woman to complete her purchase.

This may be a fairly dull—boring, actually—narrative about one episode in a typical grocery store in modern America. However, it contains many clues for improving one's civility in a country where, it seems, everyone wants *immediate* attention (aka *instant gratification*) and wants every task done *quickly*.

If empathy and respect are truly the building blocks to achieving greater civility, then we can quickly learn a few valuable lessons in civility just from this one scenario. Assuredly, the customer didn't do anything wrong—unless growing older and being frail are faults! She did not deliberately delay nor hurt anyone in any way with her delicate condition. She was simply one more customer who deserves consideration and appreciation, like all store patrons, regardless of her ability to move faster!

Meanwhile, how can we fix a broken society caused by selfishness, rudeness, and lack of compassion in our daily activities? We certainly can't remain a healthy and peaceful democratic country when so many people inwardly—and, sometimes, outwardly—are angry. These individuals are angry because of what they see in others as an out-of-control focus on their own needs and wants. Such angry people also loathe those who have a total disregard for how their behavior adversely affects the people around them.

We, as American citizens, must ensure our level of citizenship is equivalent to our level of civility. Just like people who realize that real change begins with themselves, *we* must have the courage to demonstrate, with our increased civility, the value and sanctity of caring for all those we encounter.

The United States of America has been known, since its inception, as a country with a big heart and full of people with warmth, kindness, and generosity. But, unfortunately, we have become too complacent and have relied far too long on our long-standing reputation as one of the biggest, best, and most benevolent countries in the world.

For our country to remain a leading nation and an outstanding model of a truly civilized and harmonious society, we need to work much, much harder to restore the civility we have lost in recent years. It is time we truly internalize the belief the United States of America became a *great* country because millions and millions and millions of citizens, for over 200 years, worked incredibly hard to make it so. Certainly, they could never have accomplished all they did without a powerful sense of civility towards others!

> *"America is great because she is good. If America ceases to be good, America will cease to be great."*
> —**Alexis de Tocqueville**, from Democracy in America, 1835[17]

There are no easy answers or remedies to fix the broken parts in today's America. But, like so many problems

---

[17] Alexis-Charles-Henri-Maurice Clérel de Tocqueville was a French political thinker and historian, most famous for his work Democracy in America. He visited the United States of America in 1831 and was impressed with the warmth and friendliness of so many Americans he met throughout different regions of the country.

we have faced before, we must first admit we have a problem. Certainly, our humility and openness will help us find the ways to be whole again.

How, for example, is legally breaking up any family—including those who seek asylum or even *illegal* immigrants in this country—good for America and our image of one big diverse American family? More specifically, dividing families and separating children from their parents for lengthy periods will create new and lengthy problems for our nation. These problems, no doubt, will tear at the fabric of American life in innumerable ways: traumatized children, juvenile delinquency, poor relationships with our international neighbors, and unimaginable costs related to resettlement of orphaned and abandoned children, adult homelessness, drug and alcohol abuse, and violence.

In the same way, what can we do to honor and reward the soldiers who do not possess any citizenship, and yet, have served in the United States Armed Forces? These men and women protected and defended us from our enemies while placing themselves in grave danger numerous times. They have done these things knowing they could lose their lives or severely injure their minds and bodies for the rest of their lives.

Why are these American patriots a danger to our current domestic life? What more do they have to do or be to prove their allegiance to the United States? Finally, what *logical* reason can serve for deporting these brave and honorable individuals to countries with which they no affiliation or any common bond?

~~~~~

In a similar way, we seem to discount the good works and valuable contributions made to our communities and states by ordinary citizens. These citizens, many of whom are older, impoverished financially, and ill with debilitating health conditions or diseases through no fault of their own, have led exemplary lives in so many ways.

For years, they have been active in their communities: raising money for charitable causes time and time again; helping build and maintain beautiful parks in which children can play and adults can relax; shopping frequently in their neighborhood stores to strengthen the local economy; donating their time and effort to volunteer organizations; tutoring students in schools; reading to seniors at nursing homes; and teaching their children to be productive, law-abiding, and outstanding citizens in myriad ways.

Most of all, they have not caused harm to their communities in any manner because they have continually obeyed laws; maintained their homes and yards so they are clean, attractive, and neat; have not disturbed their neighbors or blighted their neighborhood in any way; have obeyed driving laws while operating their motor vehicles; have paid their share of local, state, and federal taxes; and have not, in any way, taken anything from any government body that was not legally theirs.

Despite all of these wonderful and meaningful signs of their good citizenship (which, collectively, save our communities and country millions and millions of dollars annually), certain political groups and individuals are vehemently opposed to assisting these peaceful and productive citizens. For example, these unbending political groups and inflexible individuals resist offering affordable healthcare to these men and women so they will not have to worry endlessly about their future health needs; their basic financial security; and their place in the world as they grow older or weaker.

Consequently, we Americans need to be careful about the extent to which we emphasize the unity, generosity, and harmony of the United States in our parades, proclamations, and presidential campaigns. These signs of American goodness ring hollow to an untold number of people who are having an enormous difficulty fulfilling their most fundamental healthcare needs. So, the question remains: How can we honestly feel completely proud, contented, and satisfied when we continue to deny millions of our kind and honorable citizens the basic healthcare (and dignity) they deserve?

When one considers everything these patriotic citizens, from all levels of society, have done to ensure the great stability and optimistic spirit of America, it should be clear we owe them an affordable healthcare program whose signature qualities are respect and affirmation. As the late and very much-admired statesman US Senator John McCain (R) might say about our delay in offering affordable healthcare to all Americans, "My friends, we are better than this!"

Let's be honest about the last few years in the United States. We have seen many changes as a nation, both good and bad. Frankly, we can do better—much better—than we, as a nation, have done recently. But doing better means returning to a civility that is kind and authentic.

We are definitely at a crossroads in this country. What we think, what we expect, and, of course, what we do as American citizens to improve civility throughout our country will have a massive impact on our future as a nation.

As a result, we must ask ourselves, do we forge ahead in an arrogant, bombastic, and insensitive manner, or do we become a more humble, peaceful, and considerate nation once again? The answer is, quite simply, inside each of us.

Chapter 3
Genuine Listening: The Path to Understanding and Compromise

As adults, we are expected to pass onto our children and all other young people the manners we learned as children. This transfer of polite behavior then ensures families and communities have a sense of responsibility towards others. In this way, we promote a society of caring citizens who are humble, kind, and fair-minded. Such a transfer of manners also encourages citizens to appreciate each other's individual identity and background.

Civility, as we learned as children, is more than just remembering to say "thank you" or "pardon me" in social situations. It is a principle of responsibility that implies every action we take, in some way, has an effect on all of those around us—either now or later. So, to be exemplary citizens, we must always remain considerate and aware of the people—friends, family, strangers—with whom we interact every day.

We wrote *Making Civility Great Again* to help restore civility in all discussions and activities, especially those related to politics. (We're looking at you US Congressional Representatives, Senators, and Mr. President!) We strongly believe we Americans can eliminate our national anxiety, anger, and frustration by solving our mutual political problems in a more empathetic, respectful, and constructive manner. This approach likewise requires us to adopt (or, in some cases, restore) the manners and behavior that, for so long, have been fundamental to building a productive and nurturing American society.

How many times have you heard a person use one of these statements to explain his or her frustration with other people?

"It was a lack of communication"

"Who do they think they are?

"I can't believe people think like that!"

"I am so sick of those people and their narrow views!"

"I don't discuss politics anymore with my family."

"These people are ruining our country!"

"No one stands on principles anymore!"

All the preceding emotional outbursts have a common link: each indicates a significant breakdown in communicating well with others. It's true. When you don't communicate properly, you risk incorrect information, misunderstandings, divisiveness, stereotypes, lack of rapport, hurt feelings, and a host of other problems. All of your communication with others, to have value, must be *heard, understood, accepted,* and *acted upon.*

You are engaged in some form of communication (reading, writing, speaking, and listening) every day. Moreover, you are either a sender or a receiver of messages at any given moment.

It is your responsibility as a sender of messages to communicate as clearly as you can and then to check for the recipient's understanding. In the same way, as you receive messages, it is your responsibility to listen *actively* and ensure you receive the speaker's message as it was intended.

The following conversation (between Senator Barrow and his administrative assistant, Amanda) reveals how the speaker and listener successfully fulfill their respective responsibilities as effective communicators.

> *"Amanda, I'd like you to take care of three things while I'm away from my office this afternoon. First, please call Senator Fleming, and tell her I'll join her for breakfast at 9 am tomorrow at the Mayflower Hotel. Also, be sure my passport is up to date considering I'll be travelling to Ireland in June to meet with the Irish president. Additionally, I'd like you to edit and comment on the speech I will be presenting Friday afternoon at the Veterans of Foreign Wars convention. I left a copy of the speech in your in-basket. Please provide me with written edits and comments and place them on my desk by 6 pm."*

> *"Yes, Senator Barrow. I'll take care of your concerns. I'll be certain this morning to confirm your 9 am breakfast appointment tomorrow with Senator Fleming. Also, I'll check on your passport to ensure it's up to date for your June trip to Ireland. Of course, I'll also review your speech for the VFW convention. Then, I'll place my written edits and comments on your desk before 6 pm today. Is there anything else you would like me to do on your behalf right now?"*

"No, that's it. Thanks, Amanda."

Ideally, you move easily back and forth from one communication role to the other during a conversation, discussion, or meeting, recognizing the responsibilities each role entails. You will naturally develop effective and efficient communication skills over time once you have committed to making such an effort.

However, you must initially be a skillful and productive listener to become a competent speaker. You will have a solid foundation for your verbal communication after you have first listened as intently as possible. Together your outstanding speaking and listening skills will enhance all of your personal, public, and professional relationships

It is also critically important for you to recognize the immediate value of perfecting your listening skills as a step towards improving your level of civility. Unfortunately, few people in America today seem motivated by this knowledge—and it shows in so many spheres of our national life!

People of all ages throughout the country lament the absence of quality communication as evidenced by the decrease of productivity in our workplaces, lack of neighborliness in our communities, and the decline in civility in our daily interactions. All of these losses derive, in in one way or another, from a failure of solid listening skills.

Even more tragic for all of us, little is being done to correct the listening deficiencies in our country. For example, very few grade schools and high schools throughout the United States have formal classes in listening skills. Yet, teachers in schools deliver so much information *orally* to students who have not learned to listen effectively. This may be a major reason many students don't—or can't—master basic skills. If these students haven't learned to listen well, how can they nourish their skills in reading, writing, and speaking!

It's extremely important for you to improve *your* listening skills if you want to contribute to a peaceful, nurturing, and civil society. You will also discover, as you perfect your listening skills, that excellent listening will become a goal unto itself. Then, as you process information, meet new people, and analyze demanding social situations, your honed listening skills will guarantee your capability as a communicator navigating the complex roles of citizen, family member, friend, or coworker.

None of us was born a good listener, but you can learn sound listening skills. Good listening further helps you to communicate more effectively and enrich all of your relationships in school, at home or work, and throughout your community. In fact, listening is one skill you can develop in your personal life, and, subsequently, use in every other area of your life. The more listening you do, the more proficient your listening ability will be!

Listening is not a skill you acquire automatically if you expect to be an exceptional communicator, you must practice and reinforce your listening techniques. There are four vital questions you must consider each time you engage in a listening situation:

When should I listen and when should I speak?

To what and to whom should I listen?

What should I listen for?

How much listening should I do?

Bear in mind, too, your qualitative answer to each of these questions will have noteworthy influence on your success as a listener.

Of the four major areas of language development—*listening*, *speaking*, *reading*, and *writing*—listening is considered the first and most basic by education and mental health experts. It is the cornerstone of all human learning and communication. Think for a moment. Which of the language development skills does an infant learn first? Without a continual refinement of your listening ability, you will face even greater difficulties in acquiring other learning skills.

Listening well is certainly not easy! It is a set of processes that needs to be learned, cultivated, and nurtured throughout your lifetime. These processes are composed of the following entities:

- Sensing what is said to you
- Interpreting the meaning of a message directed towards you
- Evaluating the message you receive
- Storing the message as valuable information
- Responding (immediately or at some future point) to the message you receive

Often, these steps are not all completed at the same time. You might hear all the words in a conversation but fail to interpret or respond properly. Or you might think a particular idea of one speaker is insightful and has great merit, yet you do not act on the idea for a week or even longer. Or you may not act upon the idea at all because you think it's too complicated or difficult to execute.

In today's world, the accurate communication of information and ideas can readily determine your success or that of the group to which you belong. Imprecise or ambiguous communication, on the other hand, can lead to major misunderstandings that are damaging to your image and to the image of your organization.

Consider, too, how often you hear people make assertions similar to these:

> "I never heard you say anything about that."
>
> "He (or she) is so traditional and just doesn't want to listen to different views."
>
> "I simply cannot stand talking with that person!"
>
> "Obviously, you weren't listening well."
>
> "We have clearly reached a dilemma in our communication"

If you are regarded as a poor listener, you can appear apathetic, uncooperative, arrogant, and even condescending to others. Nonetheless, you can, with practice, vastly improve your listening so you become a more perceptive and empathetic listener.

Your genuine desire in *wanting* to become a better listener will serve you well as you strive for this goal. In addition, one of the best ways to increase your listening skills is to emulate the listening behaviors you most admire in others. You will notice, too, outstanding listeners demonstrate patience, respect, and clear nonverbal communication to ensure the accuracy of the messages they receive.

Interestingly, research indicates you listen effectively,

on average, only twenty-five percent of the time. You remember initially what was just said, but your retention rate drops quickly after that point. Also, for about forty-eight hours, you remember fifty percent of what you have heard during a conversation. Eventually, your retention rate drops to twenty-five percent.[18] Then, your listening decreases the longer the time elapses from your original discussion with another person.

Many experts estimate half of our education is spent learning to communicate. Amazingly, we spend little of this time learning to develop our listening skills. The following figures not only tell us about the quantity of time devoted to acquiring better communication skills; they clearly indicate the emphasis (or lack thereof) placed on listening skills while we are being formally educated.

During our formal education, we spend nearly forty percent of our communication skills development learning to read; thirty-five percent of our communication skills development learning to write; twenty-four percent of our communication skills development learning to speak; and one percent of our communication skills development learning to listen. When one thinks about how much of our education (especially in grade school and high school) involves listening to others, it is astonishing that only one percent of our time is spent developing this crucial skill. Is it any wonder then, later in life, several men and women struggle to achieve success because they don't listen well!

Such a deficiency in listening undoubtedly is also a reason civility is so lacking in contemporary America.

---

[18] Dick Lee and Delmar Hatesohl, "Listening: Our Most Used Communication Skill," University of Missouri Extension, 1993

Genuine civility requires people to be attentive and courteous so they communicate with others accurately and diplomatically. But this requirement also *assumes* people have been *taught* to listen intently, objectively, and empathetically!

Never forget that sincere listening is much more than a tremendous communication device. It is a wonderful gift you can give to anyone at any time, no matter who you are. It doesn't cost you a cent, but it is priceless to your communication partner as a gesture of respect and validation.

As you continue on your path to increased civility, you will invariably see how important good listening is to the process. You will learn, too, how powerful nonverbal communication and the phrasing of positive messages can be in showing your genuine civility to others.

In addition, you will discover a fourth component that is essential to a civil approach in face to face communication: the art of compromise. More than any area of communication, compromise appears to be the hardest for people to achieve. The lack of compromise is evident in so many areas of our society: business, law enforcement, religion, legal courts, and community meetings to cite several examples.

Compromise, too, is very much needed in American politics today. Just look at the large obstacles facing our government because certain people and groups will not compromise on a legion of issues. Why is compromise such a difficult goal to achieve in the political arena? Millions of American citizens want an answer to this question as they witness the inertia of their elected leaders in Congress and others in the US government. To say healthy communication is desperately needed between and among our government leaders is definitely an understatement!

How did we even get to this point? Were we misled by those who now serve as members of Congress and as President? Did we place too much trust in the promises made to us by these people as candidates? Or were we just not paying close enough attention to the messages they conveyed to us?

One thing is certain in the current political climate. The art of compromise is sorely missing in the dialogue and decisions of those elected to represent us. Because of this deep void, we currently have an incredible amount of unresolved issues, unmet needs, and underserved Americans in communities in every part of the United States.

It is unconscionable, of course, that all worthwhile American politicians would not fervently embrace the powerful art of compromise when collaborating with their political colleagues. At its heart, politics is a process of sharing and debating ideas, policies, and actions that will benefit and enhance the daily lives of all Americans. It is also a process of give and take, and, often, sacrificing a little to get a lot when personal viewpoints or individual goals collide.

During the last two decades, the art of compromising in the USA seems to have devolved into a sense of "failure," "giving in under duress," or "not being tough enough" or "not being smart enough" to accomplish a specific goal. This may be the result of inexperienced or strident politicians and political parties who *refuse* to be cooperative with those outside their party to achieve successful and substantial outcomes of any sort. Or it could be these particular individuals are exceptionally angry with the direction in which our country has moved. So, they absolutely cannot deal rationally or logically with others to take even minute steps to develop a better and stronger America.

There was indeed a time, not long ago, when politics was a noble profession in America. Though you might have been a Democrat, Republican, or Independent, you recognized that your political opponents wanted to reap many of the same benefits for your fellow Americans as you did. You simply believed your strategy for achieving these benefits was just more relevant and effective than that of your opponent.

Both you and your political peer could debate, argue, and be extremely far apart on an issue during the day while knowing full well you could—and would—resume your warm relationship once the workday ended. So, it was not unusual for the two of you to be seen enjoying cocktails and dinner or some other social event later in the evening.

Yes, you each had your own strong convictions or reasons for supporting an explicit piece of legislation or adhering to a certain political philosophy. But you remained collegial with each other and never allowed your politics to destroy your friendship or rapport.

There is a wealth of stories about political adversaries—legends really—who, despite their huge political differences, remained close friends throughout their careers. One need only to conduct brief research to learn that Thomas 'Tip" O'Neill (D), Speaker of the House of Representatives for over ten years, and Ronald Reagan (R), the fortieth President of the United States of America, were great friends and often concluded their workday with a few hearty cocktails and much lively conversation.

~~~~~

Many of us Americans—young and old from myriad cultural, religious, racial, and socioeconomic backgrounds—don't understand how we arrived at a place where we cannot even broach topics of a political nature with certain members of our family. For years, we had a great rapport with these relatives that led us to discuss political topics with a mutual respect, relaxed attitude, and a sincere interest in learning about—and from—each other's viewpoints.

Now, all these years later, we are at an impasse where we can't discuss the most basic issues, related to any part of American political life, with the people we have loved and admired for a long, long time. It's sad we can't share our honest feelings about current events involving the United States government because so much of who we are and what we believe are tied into our daily lives as American citizens.

Though it may be a cliché, "the personal is the political"[19] has never had so much relevancy for us as it does today. In fact, a large number of us are equally convinced

---

[19] The phrase was popularized by the publication of a 1969 essay by feminist **Carol Hanisch** under the title "The Personal is Political" in 1970,[4] but she disavows authorship of the phrase. No person in the feminist movement has claimed authorship of the phrase. **Steinem** has likened claiming authorship of the phrase to claiming authorship of "World War II."

the opposite is true as well: "the political is the personal" because who we are and what we do (and can do) with our lives every day have everything to do with the kind of citizens we are and become in this great democracy of ours.

This philosophy is probably why, for the last few years, conversations—over the phone or in person—between certain relatives in innumerable families have been limited to topics, such as the weather, updates on other family members, descriptions of daily activities, home and landscape improvements, recent purchases, and so forth.

So, in many ways, we Americans have reached a point at which we can no longer grasp and appreciate each other's views. There are numerous explanations for this situation in America today. Nonetheless, it would be wise for all of us to consider the truthfulness in the familiar adage "If a person doesn't stand for something, he (or she) will fall for anything."

Unfortunately, we have spent precious little time talking about our innermost thoughts, feelings, and beliefs pertaining to potentially controversial topics—immigration reform; religion; the lack of progress in the United States Congress; the questionable behavior of our President; the many fine qualities (and there *are* many to recall, regardless of your political affiliation) of former well-known political figures; the intolerance and disrespect for marginalized groups in our country and around the world; the conflicts in the Middle East; Russia's influence in American politics; the tragedies brought on by gun-toting terrorists; the disproportionate incarceration of African-Americans in our prisons; the financial benefits given to the 1% of Americans who are the wealthiest people in the United States of America; the blatant disregard for the poor and needy people in our society; and so many more critical and consequential matters that, in one way or another, affect *all of us* and affect our daily lives as American citizens.

Throughout American history, there have been countless disagreements between groups of people that have resulted in major schisms, mutual intolerance, and tremendously bloody violence. One needs only to recall the Civil War (or the War between the States) in the United States, from 1861 to 1865, to realize that huge differences in philosophy and thought can lead to rabid behavior towards others—even members of the same family.

But it is not too late for American citizens to redouble their efforts to understand one another and reach a compromise about matters of joint importance. We must first start by fully listening to others and *seriously* considering what is said to us—and how it is said to us—before we offer our response. Next, we must actively listen to others and not seek material gain, power, or convenience from our conversations with others. Finally, we must honestly, assertively, and diplomatically endorse the political views that will best benefit the neediest among us as well as our loved ones and the country we all cherish, the United States of America

We can do these things, of course, if we treat our listening habits as vital to our health—and to our nation's health! With this approach, we will once again create a spirit of trust and cooperation among our fellow citizens. When millions and millions of Americans adopt skilled listening as essential to one's citizenship responsibilities, we will truly have created a movement that, in time, becomes a culture of courtesy and cooperation.

Chapter 4
Beware of Labels, Loaded Words, and Lax Listening Filters

A large part of our incivility may stem from the preconceived notions we Americans ascribe to people whom we believe are different from us. Sometimes, we refer to these people as "those people" or "the other." More often, though, we attach a label to specific persons or groups as a way to identify them. It seems, too, there are far more labels to describe people who are different from each other than there were even two or three decades ago.

There are numerous labels today to describe a group or individual in a general (and not fully accurate) way. For example, terms like *redneck, red state, Islamic fundamentalist, evangelical Christian, bully, conservative Republican, liberal Democrat, moderate Republican, moderate Democrat, ultraconservative, Coastal Elites, Bible thumper, NRA member, transgender person, cisgender person*, and so many more indicate a particular group or person, but hardly describe the subtle and more specific nuances found in each.

Rarely, too, are these terms understood or described in *exactly* the same way by two people. So, there is a strong possibility that more confusion, misunderstandings, and, yes, impatience and annoyance will ensue when people try to have a vigorous discussion of any topic or event. The result? A weakening of bonds between individuals and a strengthening of fear and distrust of other people who have dissimilar cultures, attitudes, and ideas. In addition, speaking in generalities about distinct groups is dangerous because it often blurs reality, conveys inaccurate information, and evades facts during a conversation.

~~~~~

Everybody has their own notion of what a term or word indicates so, of course, confusion results while people are expressing their opinions during a discussion. We take for granted that certain words, references, or categories in American culture are mutually construed among people engaged in conversations. In an equivalent way, we listen to people promoting their opinions or positions on radio or television—or via other media formats—and assume they attach the same meaning to words as we do.

And we frequently learn the opposite is true. As a result, we face some unexpected results: voting for a candidate who doesn't truly share our views or goals; arguing with our children because they didn't understand exact boundaries or deadlines we set for them; agreeing to help a friend without specifying the limits or expectations for our involvement; or misunderstanding or misreading a particular overture from a person about the status of our personal or professional relationship.

Though the meaning of words may seem obvious to you when speaking in the same language with another person, it is essential for you to ensure you and your communication partner are looking at any single message in the same way. First of all, be certain each of you knows how the other interprets a word, statement, concept, policy, guideline, or instruction. Secondly, always repeat to each other the points you have covered or agreed upon together. Naturally, a proper tone of voice and positive body language can—and will—add clarity to any distinct oral message or impression you wish to convey to another person.

~~~~~

Many times, a person's cultural background, educational experiences, religious and political views, and knowledge of current events play a huge part in the person's interpretation of many words used in American conversations every day. Consequently, the following terms are often defined or interpreted distinctly by different people:

Abortion	Freedom of speech
Addicted	Gay rights
Anarchist	Gun control
Assault	Honesty
Asylum seeker	Immoral
Bible thumper	Islamic fundamentalist
Big government	Liberal Democrat
Blue state	Libertarian
Born-again Christian	Loyalty
Bully	Lie

Chain migration
Cisgender person
Civil disobedience
Civil rights
Close friend
Coastal elites
Collusion
Conservative Republican
Conspiracy
Corporate welfare
Courage
Cult
Death penalty
Domestic violence
Dysfunctional
East Coast liberal
Emotional abuse
Enemies of the people
Entitlement programs
Evangelical Christian
Fake news
Fanatic

Middle class
Moderate Democrat
Moderate Republican
NRA member
Patriot
Pornography
Presidential
Pro-choice
Pro-life
Rape
Red state
Redneck
Religious
Sexual offender
Socialist
Spineless
Traitor
Transgender person
Transsexual
Transvestite
Treason
Ultraconservative

Keep in mind some people attach great emotional meaning to certain words. If a person has very intense views about particular terms, such as pro-choice or pro-life, the individual may associate either of these with powerful images, feelings, and judgments. That's why you must be aware that these words, when uttered by people with strong convictions, can escalate both the tempo and zeal of a discussion. Always make sure you and your communication partner have a mutual understanding of these words to ensure your conversation is clear, accurate, and fruitful.

Let's say you and a friend are discussing religious views. Your friend makes the remark, "It's hard to listen to a person describe his religious views when he's a fanatic about his beliefs." So, you ask the person, "What, in your opinion, is a *fanatic*? Your friend responds, "Well, a fanatic is a person with extreme views who doesn't allow any flexibility in his thinking." Then you say, "That's interesting. I always apply the word *fanatic* to a person who is both rigid in his attitudes *and angry* that others don't look at things the way he does." Obviously, a discussion is far more pleasant and productive whenever participants share their understanding of certain words that could otherwise be interpreted in unusual ways.

~~~~~

Additionally, people quickly establish barriers to sound communication based on whether they initially like or dislike a person. This is a very shortsighted way to deal with the countless people you are bound to meet in your personal and professional life. Realistically, if you withhold your judgments of a person and try to learn more about his or her background and personality, you may find the person to be remarkably interesting and appealing on many levels.

Just because, at first, you don't like someone, you shouldn't underestimate him or her. The very person whom you may initially dislike could well turn out be the person who helps you discover unusual success, comfort, and joy in your life. In fact, that same person could be the reason your life takes a major turn towards greater self-fulfillment! Perhaps using this strategy to observe the American landscape today (especially in the areas of politics, religion, and race) could increase your understanding of the attitudes and behaviors of those whom you consider much unlike you.

You might think your dislike of a person is reason enough to disagree with his or her views no matter how insightful they may be. Quite frankly, disliking and disagreeing with a person are not mutually exclusive. You undoubtedly have known numerous people in your life with whom you have disagreed about a policy, law, philosophy, or other matter. But you still found much to admire about the person, especially because you shared many common values, namely, honesty, empathy, integrity, and a respect for facts.

Not surprisingly, you may—and often do—vehemently disagree with friends about specific issues, viewpoints, and opinions. However, you continue to enjoy and appreciate the company of these friends because of similar core values. You are confident then your dissimilar views will not hurt your warm relationship because a rapport, built on like-minded attitudes, already exists between you.

This is the crux of a new theory we now refer to as the Double D Theory of Civility. Does your dislike of another person automatically cause you to disagree with his or her views? Does your disagreement with a person's views cause you unequivocally to dislike him or her?

Dealing with your family members and other loved ones creates a unique challenge when considering the Double D Theory of Civility. You, in all probability, are comfortable with the personalities and speech patterns, including their tone of voice, of those closest to you. In all likelihood, you are much more willing to be patient with these people and tolerant of their views (even those in complete opposition to yours) than you would be with strangers.

It's natural, too, for you to expect consideration and respect at all times from everyone. Nevertheless, whenever you feel like any individual, not to mention a relative or friend, is starting to criticize your ideas or beliefs in a mocking or disparaging way, it's time for you to end the conversation! You are not bound to engage in any conversation with *anyone* who belittles or ridicules you or your thoughts in any way! (See pages 238 to 247 about angry confrontations.)

Sometimes, it's incredibly difficult to have safe, sane, and sensible conversations with people who are a big part of your life or whom you have loved deeply for years. But you have to live with *yourself* and respect yourself enough to recognize that great and lasting relationships are based on mutual trust and respect.

So, in the end, only you can decide how much you want to share your thoughts with people around you. Conversely, only you can decide how much you are willing to accommodate the opinions of these people to maintain a healthy relationship with them. Ultimately, authentic camaraderie with other people is not based on mere agreement or identical reactions to the world and events surrounding us. It is built on mutual openness, trust, and respect.

We have, for over thirty years, successfully conducted communication skills workshops for corporations, nonprofit organizations, and community-based groups. Each workshop has been composed of people from many diverse backgrounds. These programs dramatically improved the interactions of people as they speak and listen to each other. So, we clearly understand how a person's *approach* to another individual in face to face communication has everything to do with the durability and growth of that relationship.

For example, a number of years ago, we were conducting a listening skills workshop for a hotel in Chicago that is part of a worldwide organization. The participants in this class were all managers, men and women from many countries, including the United States, Venezuela, Switzerland, Iraq, Germany, and Austria.

One activity involved reviewing the behavior of three people in a workplace situation and ranking the individuals according to how much they were responsible for the problems mentioned in the written narrative we provided to the participants. The essence of this workplace situation was whether one manager was obligated to report negative information about another manager (who was also his friend) to a high-level executive. We had deliberately included loaded words in the narrative that could be interpreted in many ways like *lied, friendship, truth, anguish, fair, guilt ridden, retribution,* and so forth to stimulate a group discussion. To say the class engaged in a lively discussion would be an understatement!

We all learned an important lesson that day. One's political and social background (including exposure to a particular form of government and legal system within a country) can have a tremendous effect on an individual's future communication and decision-making as he or she interacts with others.

What was very revealing was how the workshop participants reacted to the idea of reporting the negative behavior of a colleague. Some people who were raised outside of the United States, said they would *never* divulge information about an illegal or improper act of a professional colleague who was also a friend. Others, who were born and raised in the United States, were adamant the manager *must* report such an act to a high-level company executive because the company was paying the manager's salary! Still other participants (some raised in the United States and some not) were extremely uncomfortable with making such a decision at all.

Another truly valuable lesson the entire class acquired that day was the realization of the wide variety of meanings people attach to certain words as well as the level of importance they place on these words (such as the loaded words mentioned earlier). So, it is a reminder to all of us to make sure, when speaking with people in any professional or personal situation, the words and terms we use are equally understood by all communication partners.

Furthermore, we believe, from the first moment we encounter a person, we become immediately aware of the way they express their message to us—via their words, tone of voice, and most of all, nonverbal communication. If our initial impression of the person's communication *approach* is negative in any way, the power of his or her message to influence us in a positive way is severely limited.

Consider for example, a person who initially addresses you in a manner that is self-centered, conceited, narcissistic, or dishonest. Then, as he speaks, you realize his statements are utterly lacking in empathy, respect for various beliefs and traditions, support of facts he cites, and a general disregard of all people he disdains. What would be your first impression of this person?

Very likely, as we often point out in our books and workshops, you will *shut down* as a listener. That is a natural and normal reaction for anyone. When you, as a human being, feel threatened, intimidated, or uncomfortable with a person's speech and demeanor, you automatically reject the message—no matter what it may be!

You obviously cannot have a healthy exchange of ideas with a person who ignores, mocks, or insults your basic values. Further, you will distance yourself from such people who are more interested in promoting their own views and listening only to people who agree with them. A prime opportunity is then lost for creating a meaningful discussion between two people because of one person's total self-absorption and lack of respect for his communication partner.

Before people can become effective listeners and increase their level of civility, they must understand the mental and emotional processes that heavily affect communication between human beings. These learned influences—or filters—are an intricate part of human development. Nevertheless, each person determines to what extent these processes will affect the quality of his or her communication with other people.

Filters are the thoughts and ideas that influence your judgments, decisions, behaviors, and opinions on a daily basis. You accumulate such filters from a variety of sources in your life: family history, work experiences, childhood incidents, educational opportunities, religious beliefs, and very personal (and, sometimes, traumatic) events are among these many sources.

These emotional and psychological processes, or filters, either enhance or harm your communication with others. Especially in the area of *interpreting messages* will you find filters having the power to influence how you listen to people. Therefore, depending on how you employ them, filters can expand or limit your understanding as you receive messages from your communication partners.

Once you are an adult, you have learned to use filters effectively so your contact with others is stimulating and productive. Being aware of how forcefully your filters can affect the quality of your speaking and listening will make you more flexible, accepting, and nonjudgmental in your reactions. On the other hand, either consciously or unconsciously, you may occasionally use your filters in an unfavorable way. If you employ your filters in a detrimental way, you will hamper your communication with people, be they friends, family members, colleagues, or strangers. This negative communication can, in time, create a tense or angry atmosphere that alienates you from others.

Of course, not everyone is influenced, or influenced in the same way, by the same filters. Depending on your experiences that stretch all the way back to your infancy, you may place great significance on certain people, events, and things that are or were part of your life.

As you grow older and move through life, these same people, events, and things filter your thinking and the innumerable choices and decisions you make. The challenge then is to analyze the filters you use and employ them to enrich your listening proficiency—and not destroy it—as you strive to communicate dynamically with everyone in your life.

Common Filters

Again, there are distinct types of filters that affect your listening on a daily basis. By looking at a number of these filters, you will see how your personal filters can make a large dent in your communication success.

Assumptions

Without knowing the facts or accurately analyzing a person, group, or a situation, what opinions do you hold about the person, group, or situation? Which of the opinions are truly superficial on your part? Have you asked yourself when and where you initially made this assumption?

Attitudes

What are your firmly held ideas that stem from both your personal and professional experiences? How do these attitudes influence your clear and accurate communication with other people? How do these same attitudes cause you to approach or avoid communicating with specific individuals?

Beliefs

What viewpoints do you retain based on your family life, religion, geographic region in which you live or were raised, ethnic culture, racial origin, and sexual identity, and so forth? Do your beliefs allow for a consideration of other ideas? Do your views encourage flexibility and logic in you?

Charisma

Are you often distracted, by your communication partner's (or a public speaker's) appearance, delivery style, persuasiveness, charming accent, or enthusiasm—and not hearing the content of the person's message? What can you do to listen closely to the *words* of a charismatic person so you understand his or her *complete* message?

Defensiveness

Do you occasionally react to a person as though you are being unfairly criticized, blamed, undermined, or threatened? What is the source of your defensive behavior? How can you prepare for not reacting defensively in future conversations and discussions with friends, family members, and colleagues?

Emotional Reactions

Do you sometimes listen emotionally instead of logically to the messages you receive? Do you focus solely on your own feelings when absorbing information from another person? How does this approach influence your overall communication and relationships with people in your daily interactions?

Expectations

What do you believe will happen, or what do you *want* to happen at work, at home, or with people you know? How do such thoughts affect your anticipation or avoidance of particular situations and events? In what ways do your expectations make you a more optimistic or pessimistic person?

Fear

Have you, at certain times, been afraid to be honest, open, or direct with other individuals because you anticipated a negative or unpleasant reaction? What made you most fearful of speaking truthfully to these people? How can you be more relaxed and optimistic when interacting with people in the future?

Hostility

Have you distorted messages because you were hearing them while you were in an angry, agitated, or highly volatile state? How did these distortions affect your self-esteem and your long-term relationships with others? What have you done to prevent such negative communication from occurring in your life today?

Images of the past, present, and future

How do you perceive your immediate world? What images of your past and future help you to be more positive (or more negative) in your outlook? Why do some images of your past occupy such a prominent place in your memory? Are certain images reoccurring often in your mind and preventing you from moving forward with optimism?

Insincerity

Are you resistant or afraid to tell others who you really are or what your genuine feelings, beliefs, and opinions are? Do you think your relationships would change if you were more open with your family members, friends, and work associates? How can you be truly sincere and authentic with people you know?

Intense feelings

What observations, experiences, situations, and values have created powerful emotions in you? How do these intense feelings affect you physically, emotionally, or psychologically? Do you ever wonder if your intense feelings cause you to overreact when communicating with others? If so, how can you keep those feelings in check?

Interests

How are you influenced by the things you find most pleasurable, relaxing, or fulfilling? What happens to your communication with people who share your interests as opposed to those who don't? Do you actively seek out people whose interests are vastly different from yours? Are you bored quickly with people who don't share your interests?

Memories

What has happened in your own life that colors and influences the information you receive from someone else? Are you prone to compare people you knew in the past with people you know now based on their similar appearance and personality? In what ways do your memories affect your level of empathy, respect, and consideration for other people?

Past experiences

How do your previous life experiences influence your behavior today? What effect do they have on your current judgments? How do these experiences continue to build confidence in you, or, conversely, to hurt or damage your self-confidence? Do you readily see a connection between your (or others') memories and current approach to life?

Physical environment

What in your physical surroundings comforts you or distracts you? Which smells, sounds, or scenes recall circumstances that were extremely pleasant or extremely upsetting for you in the past? How is your communication with other people influenced by heat, cold, noise, hunger, and other factors? What can you do to improve your physical environment for better communication with your family, friends, and colleagues?

Prejudices

What biases do you possess that stem from your family background, religion, racial identity, cultural setting, geographic region, political views, socioeconomic level, and unpleasant or negative experiences? Which of these biases are most evident in your personality today? What can you do to eliminate any of your lingering prejudices?

Selective Listening

Is it possible you hear only what you want to hear or expect to hear from another person? In the same way, do you seek ways to use this distinct information to your advantage? Have you considered the possibility you listen *selectively* to people because you are more interested in benefiting materially from a conversation than learning from it?

Status

Do you feel, at times, less powerful or influential (or more powerful or influential) than the people with whom you are communicating? How does this feeling affect the quality of your communication with people? What would make you feel equal to your communication partners in these situations?

Semantics

Have you used words during an exchange with others that only make sense to someone in a certain industry, field, occupation, political party, or advocacy group? Or have you employed phrases and slogans that mean different things to different people? What is the reason you did so? How can you avoid this mistake in the future?

Values

What strong principles do you hold that derive from your core values and beliefs, physical and cultural environment, schooling, familial bonds, and friendships? What effect do these principles have on your social interactions with other people, especially those whose views and backgrounds are quite different from yours? Are your values consistently reflected in your actions and behaviors?

~~~~~

There are many kinds of listening skills, but we continue to promote the concept of *active listening* in both personal and professional settings. In active listening, *you* have a definite responsibility as a listener. You must not only listen to a speaker's words; you must try to discern both the accurate meanings and feelings behind his or her words.

Many listening experts believe you are truly listening only when you *actively* grasp the facts and feelings in what you are hearing from others. Moreover, these experts maintain your active listening helps your communication partners while they are speaking to you.

Speakers become more composed and relaxed in delivering messages whenever they are aware of your sincere interest in the meanings and emotions underlying their messages. As you listen actively to these speakers, they process and understand their own thoughts and feelings. Your active listening then gives these speakers the confidence to deliver their entire message.

Overall, you can enhance your discussions with others by ensuring you and they are mutually applying the same meaning to key words. You can also perfect your capability as an active listener by employing all of your listening filters in productive ways that lend greater clarity and understanding to the messages you send and receive.

Most important, you must remain aware effective communication with others is indeed a two-way street requiring each person to listen and speak as though everything depends on this process. You are clearly destined for a reputation of exemplary communication when you approach all of your face to face situations with this attitude.

Chapter 5
Know When and Why You Are Not Listening—and What You Can Do About It

Know When and Why You Are Not Listening

You have dusted the cobwebs out of your brain, you have promised yourself you'll be more mannerly, and you have checked your filters at the door before a potentially heated discussion.

You've shared some of your views on the subject at hand. It's a subject for which you have passion.

So, you're good to go…. Or maybe not.

The voices in your mind grow louder until finally you decide you are right, and the other person can only be wrong. You feel the heat rising in your body. "Stop!" A voice inside your head screams. "Stop believing you can only be right, and the other person is wrong. Stop rehearsing your responses and really listen. You might actually learn something, and decide the other person is right and you are wrong." Meanwhile, you would do well to consider the following nuggets of communication wisdom:

- To become a more skilled listener on any level, you should be aware of the distinct situations in which you listen passively, halfheartedly, or not at all. Excellent communication requires you practice your listening skills at all times, even when you find it exceedingly difficult to do so. It also requires you to be a more patient and understanding human being as both a private and public citizen.

- You can further cultivate your reputation as an expert listener by making a determined effort to rid yourself of the emotional problems that tie you to poor and ineffective communication habits. This, of course, necessitates a deliberate attempt to use your listening filters in a constructive way. It also demands you eliminate all the stereotypes, generalities, and preconceived notions in your mind that frequently clutter clear thinking and lead to subjective listening.

- You must also keep in mind your environment, at any given time, affects the quality of your listening. Certain noises, physical factors (heat, cold, hunger), unpleasant odors, and the level of comfort in a particular place may have the potential to interfere with your ability to listen easily and fully to your communication partner. If this is the case, you should ensure a setting that is conducive to sound listening. The quality of your listening skills, otherwise, will always be dependent on your moods, minor annoyances, and implicit biases.

Know What You Can Do About Not Listening

You can only remove your listening barriers after you have identified the specific times—and the reasons why—you are not listening efficiently. Once you have discovered these situations and how you create them, you can apply powerful solutions to change your listening habits and initiate meaningful communication with everyone. There is a variety of methods you can use, depending on your individual limitations, to increase your influence as a listener.

To discover innovative and practical answers to your own communication challenges, it is necessary to involve yourself in the dynamics of building greater rapport with your friends, family, and professional colleagues. Successful rapport building requires you to acknowledge the unique personality and strengths of every person with whom you interact.

It also requires you to consider the unique differences of these people so your communication with each person is always open, respectful, and authentic. In this way, you fortify personal and professional relationships that remain satisfying, nurturing, and harmonious through both pleasant and difficult periods.

~~~~~

So, what can you do to communicate well with everyone—even those whose views appear intolerant, disagreeable, or even abhorrent to you? The answer to this question cannot be stated easily nor fully to most people's satisfaction.

First of all, you must remind yourself, as you communicate with others, all people have the right to express their opinion, view, belief, comment, or reaction at any appropriate time. You, of course, also have the right *not* to listen to anyone's opinion, view, belief, comment, or reaction at any time.

Now let's assume you have chosen to listen to a person whose views, in all likelihood, are vastly different from yours. Moreover, you've decided you want to listen thoughtfully to this person explain or describe his or her views in greater detail about a specific subject. The topic could be about politics, sexual or gender orientation, sports, immigration, educational philosophy, or any other matter.

Because you're determined to listen to this person, what do you need to ensure a healthy and harmonious dialogue with him or her? What do you do or say when the person expresses ideas that are definitely intellectually contrary to yours? Equally important, how can you remain emotionally calm if this person uses a condescending tone of voice, poor examples to illustrate a particular opinion, or inaccurate information that makes you feel unsettled, uncomfortable, frustrated, or angry?

~~~~~

It is depressing to examine the level of incivility in politics in contemporary America. This is an area in which a great many Americans have allowed outrageous behavior, baseless accusations, and vicious attacks on people's reputations to dominate their interest and to determine which person or political party they will support.

It appears, too, these people believe a politician "tells it like it is" when he or she uses coarse language or vitriol to convey a point of view or an opinion. This disregard for fundamental manners in the public sphere is just one more example of a lack of self-respect and lowered expectations among our citizenry. Moreover, this display of poor behavior continues to erode the civility that once was a hallmark of worldliness and sophistication in the United States. For example, we continue to tune into TV and radio stations where political commentators routinely make accusations about people or describe others with inaccurate or blatantly false information simply to gain favor with their partisan voters.

No longer do we listen to *full* accounts of a politician's views on current issues. Nor do we listen objectively to various candidates' positions. Rather, we allow ourselves to determine the value—or validity—of a politician's statements by our *emotional* reaction to his or her views, looks, personal and professional background, or political affiliation. Worst of all, we don't seem to want or care to know how and why a candidate holds a distinct view.

Though we often realize certain information about a politician is untrue, we ignore the danger of falsehoods simply because we don't like the person or his or her political party! In other words, we quickly decide the person is wrong, misguided, or immoral without ever trying to understand the complete reasons, facts, and philosophy that are essential to the person's viewpoints or ideas.

Also dangerous are the assumptions we make about people running for office—or voters themselves—when we ponder or discuss the political leanings of people. Whether asking individuals about their views or analyzing the surveys of people in any specific demographic, we often make general assumptions about their backgrounds, culture, workplace goals, family life, religious attitudes, and a myriad of other topics.

Quite frankly, these blanket assumptions frequently include both implicit and explicit biases that skew our objectivity and accuracy of the very people's lives we are examining. This naturally can have disastrous consequences in communicating our messages to others while attempting to have these individuals embrace our political goals and philosophy. Such assumptions, because of their inherent inequality, unfairness, and prejudice, have very adverse effects on our traditionally democratic processes.

So, a basic tool for truly listening and comprehending what others say to us—and what we say to them—is a mutual understanding of the words we use in our communication. This may appear as a simplistic and obvious observation. In the United States of America, however, innumerable communication problems and barriers exist because most people fail to consider the exact meaning of words they convey to their communication partners or the words conveyed to them by other individuals. (See Chapter 4, pages 69to 70 for an extensive list of words that are interpreted in different ways by many people.)

Keep Eye Contact

Eye contact is compelling and immediate. It is so powerful that you can completely support or undermine a speaker with eye contact alone. Try bringing up a sensitive subject with someone who is rolling his or her eyes or whose eyes are glaring, squinting, or locked in an apathetic haze. How important, validated, or supported do you feel?

Whenever you communicate with someone in person, look at the speaker, and maintain solid eye contact throughout the conversation. Directing your eyes on the speaker helps you keep your mind on the message. It also encourages the speaker to continue talking and makes him or her feel more comfortable. The more you concentrate on the speaker, the less chance there is of misunderstanding the message.

With your eye contact, you clearly convey your attitude as a listener. It is critical, therefore, the quality of your eye contact reflect your interest, patience, and curiosity as you grasp the speaker's message.

It's surprising how many people are uncomfortable looking directly into a person's eyes. While responding to another person's oral communication, they look over the person's head, to the side of the person's face, or at the person's mouth. These people may feel such eye contact is an invasion of one's privacy. Others, because of their cultural background, believe direct eye contact is rude and aggressive behavior. In short, people who hold such views will do anything to avoid gazing directly into another person's eyes.

In American culture, however, focusing on the speaker's eyes is admired as a very polite and respectful gesture. Direct eye contact also reflects assertive and confident behavior of people in America.

When you're terribly interested in a person—and what he or she has to say—it's mirrored in your eyes. Your eye contact provides you with three distinct communication features beyond the verbal message you are receiving. First, you understand where your speaker is taking you from your visual observations of him or her. Second, you grasp all of the subtle nuances of your speaker's message that better enable you to evaluate its relevance for you. Third, you nurture the speaker so the person is encouraged to deliver his or her message in its entirety. This, in turn, leads to more open communication between the two of you.

Conversely, when you are simply going through the motions of listening to feign politeness, your eye contact is much less genuine, powerful, and courteous. It also sends a message to your communication partners that you aren't much interested in them or in their message. So, in a brief time, not only have you missed part or all of their message; you have also damaged your relationships with these people because of your inconsideration.

Solid eye contact then greatly increases your listening skills because the quality of your direct eye contact is in direct proportion to your interest in—and comprehension of—your communication partner's message to you. Moreover, effective eye contact conveys your respect to the speaker, deepens your grasp of the speaker's verbal and nonverbal message, and provides a bridge to more detailed communication between you and the speaker.

Pay Attention

According to some sources, a speaker talks at about 125 words a minute. Other sources indicate the average person speaks at a rate of 110 to 160 words per minute.[20]

On the other hand, our minds absorb information at a rate of 400 to 500 words per minute. Some studies even suggest a listener's mind speeds along at over 1,000 words a minute. Regardless of the sources cited, a large rate of absorption is possible because we think in *clusters* or groups of words.[21]

Keep in mind, too, the average listener's mind wanders every five to ten minutes provided the speaker is energizing and the listener is interested in the topic. A number of experts estimate our attention span may be even less. Many studies also argue most people miss about 85 percent of what is said to them. Accordingly, it is imperative you keep your mind from wandering to ensure sound listening habits.

> *You're discussing potential Congressional candidates to run in the midterm elections with the staff of your party's National Committee when suddenly you find yourself counting the number of overtime hours necessary for a down payment on a new car.*
>
> *You aren't paying attention! Back to the potential Congressional candidates.... Boom!*

---

[20] Kerrigan, Kim and Wells, Steven, Corporate Classrooms, *Get a Grip on Speaking and Listening,* Copyright 1993 by Prentice Hall.

[21] See Footnote 12.

You're daydreaming about your upcoming week in the Caribbean.

Tuning out a speaker, whether it be a friend, relative, or client and tuning in to unrelated, random thoughts is quite common—and potentially dangerous to your reputation! A public speaker, friend, or client may not be particularly interesting or dynamic, but it is your responsibility as a proficient listener to be fully present and aware when communicating with others.

Paying attention for an extended period of time takes work. It is a necessary and respectful part of any solid communication. You can train yourself to focus on something, and to stay connected to the moment. Watch and listen for words, body language, and changes in voice inflection or volume by the speaker.

Loss of attention sometimes stems from judging what you are hearing. If you don't think the speaker is competent, personable, or exciting, you may choose not to listen at all. Remember, too, your *positive* judgments of the speaker can distract you. Are you staring at the speaker's impeccably tailored clothes? Are you swept away by his or her charisma, oblivious to the fact the person's rambling thoughts have no substance or value for you or your current situation? Bother to be where you are!

Many believe our lifestyles, including a heavy dependence on technology and social media, are partly to blame for our lack of proficient listening skills. It's quick and easy to change channels when we are bored, tired, or simply not motivated to pay attention to the topic at hand.

Paying attention takes effort! Experts say it even creates physical tension in our bodies—faster heartbeat, alert body stance, and mental and physical fatigue. It's really several skills: eliminating distractions, remaining focused on the speaker's message, interpreting the speaker's body language, and reacting to his or her facial expressions

Use technology to *your* advantage. Some people in today's world look at telephones, cell phones, blackberries, computers, and Twitter as monumental interrupters of communication. However, it doesn't have to be that way!

Voice mail, for example, has become increasingly accepted in both our personal and workplace lives. So, use your voice mail to intercept calls when you are discussing an important issue with a colleague or friend. It's not only expedient; it's the courteous and professional thing to do! With voice mail, you can still answer the telephone with a cheery "hello," yet continue your discussion with another person, all the while preventing communication misunderstandings. And your voice mail message ensures you won't ever sound hurried or frustrated to your callers.

Listen for Details

Sometimes, we listen for entertainment; other times, we listen to be prepared or make judgments. At other times, we listen to help someone express their feelings. Many times, we are listening for information, facts, or ideas. often, it helps to know *in advance* what we want to get from our listening.

People process information in a variety of ways and must be prepared to absorb many pieces of data in just a few seconds. A valuable tool at your disposal is your pen.

Taking notes is highly recommended, even in informal meetings. There is no need to rely solely on your memory. Writing will help you to make sense of what you've heard and to remember it more quickly and accurately.

For example, knowing the value of good notes, you might record the following significant facts and observations during a community meeting on new trash recycling guidelines:

> *Five percent increase in volume six months in a row*
> *Mixed paper with plastic and plastic with paper—not good!*
> *All neighborhoods in the city affected*
> *Everyone is responsible*
> *If no improvement in 6 weeks,* <u>*cost doubles*</u>
> *Must do our part*
> *Pass increased cost onto households*

Most speakers, especially in a large meeting or public forum, have developed their presentation or talk from a logical outline. So, try to listen for key words or details that are included in such an outline.

Your notes are for your benefit, so develop a system of notetaking that makes sense to you. You can mark what you feel are the most important points; denote ideas about which the speaker seems extremely excited or enraged; or list any jargon you don't understand to review and research later. Any system that works for you is the best system.

In the same way, a smart phone with a voice recorder app can be a tremendous help in gathering more accurate information while listening to others, particularly during a major presentation, keynote address, or detailed report.

Naturally, in light of various laws and regulations, one must ask beforehand whether recording of the speaker's words is allowed. If it is, you have the advantage of reviewing the speaker's detailed message and breaking it down into notes to highlight all of the information that is important to you.

Don't Interrupt

There's an old saying that *the ears don't work until the tongue has expired*. Not interrupting others is essential to be an outstanding listener. Thomas Jefferson invented the dumb waiter for a simple reason. He wanted to avoid interrupting his conversations with dinner guests to speak with servants.

When people interrupt others, it's usually because they are focusing on what they want to say rather than on the words of the speaker. Interruptions are often rude and distracting, and they can cause the speaker's message to become garbled, confused, and misunderstood.

In some meetings, classes, workshops, and other group situations, speakers invite listeners to participate by asking questions as the presentation moves along. Interruptions will certainly occur during such events.

However, if you do have questions (even during a one-on-one conversation), keep them pertinent to the subject at hand. Be sure also to keep your questions generic to the group's interest when you are part of a group discussion. Questions that are unique to your personal situation should be reserved until after the presentation when you can talk with the speaker privately.

On the other hand, staying confused does not make you appear more polite or intelligent. Indeed, it places you in a risky and unprofessional position that could have unintended consequences for you and the speaker. Interruptions, when meaningful and thoughtful, are important listening techniques; when random and unnecessary, they can cause irreparable damage to open communication.

Keep an Open Mind

How many times have you heard someone say, "It was a communication problem" when describing a misunderstanding between two people? Often, the communication malfunction is the result of each person's lack of focus in either delivering or receiving a message clearly. In these situations, the communication difficulty can best be summarized with the statement, "I know you believe you understand what you think I said, but I am not sure you realize that what you understand is not what I meant."

We all have our own unique experiences, opinions, attitudes, and biases, each of which can affect the content of messages we receive from others. It's essential then you use your emotions to *understand* the speaker. If you respect the feelings and points of view of others, you will gain much more from your listening. People will also admire you for your ability to listen with an open mind, and they will be much more willing to listen to you later.

As we mentioned earlier, there are many filters that can prevent you from listening with an open mind. Another of these may be your propensity to be a *selective listener*. Consequently, you may limit your communication skills. You may sometimes hear only what you want to hear, what you agree with, or what makes you feel good. Another barrier that keeps you from listening with an open mind, at times, is your attraction to— or your dislike of—the speaker as well as people and circumstances associated with the speaker.

Just be aware your personal life experiences have the potential to affect your listening skills in negative ways. You may, for example, have a tough time respecting and validating another person as a distinct individual with his or her own values, ideas, and opinions. If so, it is crucial you continually remind yourself that no two human beings will ever think, feel, act, or react in an identical way.

~~~

Its clear numerous factors affect your ability to be a sound listener: your own biases, inattentiveness, poor eye contact, interruptions, personal tastes, and a host of other self-defeating behaviors. Yet, you have the power within you to be a much stronger listener if you can become more other-directed. As you concentrate more sharply on what people say to you, you will shed more of your personal communication biases and self-centeredness. In time, you will exhibit greater determination, focus, and empathy in listening to others and absorbing their messages completely and accurately. What all of this really entails for you is taking charge of every listening situation of which you are a part.

You need to eliminate as many distractions as possible; be entirely engaged with your communication partner; and grasp as much of the emotional, intellectual, and spiritual content of his or her message as you can. Only in this manner will you develop the habits that will lead you to be an outstanding listener.

And, yes, this is a lot of work. But the rewards for you and your personal and professional life will be endless!

Chapter 6
Connecting with People in a Positive, Productive, and Precise Way

The goal in communicating is keeping the channel between the sender and receiver as open as possible. As the receiver, you can support this process by creating a nonjudgmental, receptive environment. Be aware that your listening is a gesture of respect and validation for the speaker. There are many ways for you to stay alert and involved in a one-on-one conversation or group discussion; collectively, these methods are known as feedback techniques.

Feedback techniques are the statements you use as an involved listener to respond to a speaker. As such, they are the most powerful tools you have to sustain and enhance your communication with others when your role is that of listener. Feedback techniques further demonstrate you want to receive a speaker's message correctly and become *actively* involved in the communication process as a listener.

There are four main feedback techniques always available to you as an active listener: asking clarifying questions, restating what you have heard, responding with neutral comments, and summarizing the key points.

You use these key feedback techniques to draw more information from a speaker and become more actively involved as a listener. Furthermore, by employing feedback techniques, you acknowledge the speaker's message by posing relevant questions; by restating essential information; or, in the simplest form, by confirming his or her remarks with your appropriate responses and productive body language.

Soon, you will be having a lively and pleasant exchange because both of you are learning new things about each other. In the process, each of you will eliminate the preconceptions you might have had about the other's political leanings.

Analyzing the Four Main Feedback Techniques

Asking your communication partner clarifying questions is appropriate and helpful to guarantee accurate communication. If you don't understand some instructions, guidelines, or ideas, respect yourself and the speaker enough to say so.

When you ask a clarifying question, you indicate to your communication partner you need more information to grasp his or her full message. Sometimes, you may only need a one-word response, such as "yes" or "no." At other times, you may require a more detailed answer to remain focused on the speaker's message.

In the same way, you restate key comments made by the speaker to assure precise understanding of the words just spoken by him or her. It is also easier, by restating comments throughout a conversation, to weave a theme that assists you in comprehending and remembering the full message of your communication partner.

Inserting your neutral comments while you listen can be both beneficial and calming for the speaker, too. During natural pauses in a conversation, you encourage a speaker to continue (and you can even affirm his or her feelings or ideas) by making short, *nonjudgmental* statements. You further display your empathy with neutral comments to indicate you comprehend what the speaker is saying and are sensitive to the feelings he or she is experiencing.

Summarizing the speaker's major points, when strategically placed in a conversation or discussion, can bring an entire dialogue into focus. This summary serves to clarify, restate, and affirm the content all at once. In addition, summarizing the speaker's primary statements highlights the vital information covered during any particular exchange.

The four main feedback techniques are simple to understand but require practice to implement. The challenge is employing them effectively in our conversations and discussions with people to prove we know what they are saying!

Now, look at a description of each feedback technique that follows and its distinct features. As you review the technique and its corresponding examples, ponder the many situations in which you could utilize the same technique for more productive communication with those around you.

Remember, too, all of the following feedback techniques, used in combination, serve to validate and respect your speaker. Get in the habit of using these techniques as often as you can when you converse with others. When it is your turn to speak, you will appreciate a similar effort from the person or people listening to you.

Ask Clarifying Questions.

REASONS

- To obtain additional facts
- To help explore many sides of a problem
- To gain more detailed information
- To acquire more elaborate responses

EXAMPLES

"What exactly did the American Ambassador to Japan mean by that statement?"

"In what ways did the reporter irritate the Senator at the press conference?"

"Are these the only three issues out of twenty on which the committee members can agree?"

"Have you explained the new House bill to the entire staff?"

Restate What You Have Heard.

REASONS

- To check your meaning and interpretation with those of the other person
- To demonstrate you are listening and understand what is what said to you
- To show you understand how the person feels
- To motivate the person to analyze and discuss other aspects of the topic at hand

EXAMPLES

"You feel the President failed to represent our country during the press conference with King Guda."

"As I understand it, you plan not to seek reelection for your House seat but do plan to seek the Democratic nomination for Senator of New Mexico."

"So, you think things would only get worse if I made my dissatisfaction with the Congress known to the press?"

"In your opinion, we need to focus much more effort on eliminating the Electoral College before the 2024 presidential campaign."

Respond with Neutral Comments.

REASONS

- To indicate you are listening
- To encourage the other person to continue talking
- To validate the speaker
- To refrain from offering your opinion

EXAMPLES

"I can see how frustrated you are with the election results."

"I completely understand what you are saying about First Amendment rights."

"Please help me fully understand your views on abortion."

"Let's talk more about your reactions to the recent protests in Virginia."

Summarize the Key Points.

REASONS

- To confirm you have been listening carefully and empathetically
- To review the critical elements of a dialogue for mutual understanding of the essential points
- To bring the discussion into focus for conclusion

- To serve as a starting point for further communication

EXAMPLES

"So, you believe the two principal issues facing America today are epidemic racism and widespread poverty."

"If I follow you correctly, you think your fellow Republicans are making a big mistake remaining silent about the latest action taken by the President."

"Then, what you're planning to do is file a complaint of negligence against the EPA Cabinet Secretary and his staff."

"Therefore, you want me to be aware the most pressing issue within the Justice Department is the low morale that exists as a result of the latest policies set by the current Administration."

~~~~~

Our minds are full of information and memories recorded over a lifetime. Often, new data will trigger a memory or a thought related to a particular topic. A skilled listener puts these reflex thoughts on pause while absorbing new information.

It is not necessary to verbalize every thought that pops into your head. Some of your ideas may be entertaining or even interesting. However, they frequently detract from the main flow of your active listening.

Interruptions can be sometimes slightly annoying or blatantly rude. In these situations, the interruptions convey to the speakers they, as well as their messages, are not important. Do *your* interruptions communicate a sense of impatience? A lack of interest? An attitude of superiority? Take note of *why* you feel the need to interrupt. Regardless of their content, most interruptions are barriers to open communication.

There are some situations, of course, in which interruptions can be helpful. If you are absolutely unclear about something that the speaker has said, and your immediate understanding of that subject is critical, go ahead and interrupt in an appropriate and gentle manner. Interruptions for the sake of clarification can avert misunderstandings and can help speakers gauge the effectiveness of both their delivery and their remarks.

As with so many other communication processes, how you interrupt someone will determine further communication with that person. You should, therefore, be as tactful and diplomatic as possible when you must interrupt someone's conversation or presentation.

Be certain to apologize to the speaker for your interruption. Also, express your apology in a tone of voice that reflects both humility and empathy.

Then, focus specifically on the speaker's comments or words about which you need further clarification. It is also wise, after the speaker has responded to you, to mention how his or her reply has lessened your confusion (or, conversely, has increased your understanding) of a particular topic.

Consider the following example in which a United States Senator interrupts the Secretary of Homeland Security who is presenting information about the reunification of immigrant parents and children. It clearly demonstrates an appropriate and suitable interruption during a discussion.

Secretary of Homeland Security

The parent/child reunification program will go into effect within ninety days.

Senator

Excuse me, please, for my interruption, but I'm confused. I thought we were reuniting children with their parents within thirty days.

Secretary of Homeland Security

Well, we had discussed the possibility of reuniting the children with their parents within thirty days, but, after we met with our field personnel, we felt strongly we needed to perform diligent background checks on the parents. We need ninety days to complete all of them. We will reunite individual parents and their children if their background checks are completed earlier than ninety days.

Senator

Thank you for pointing out that information to me. I had no idea the background checks could take as long as ninety days to complete. Now, I have a better understanding of this process.

~~~~~

Open-Ended Questions Add Life to Your Conversations

People who develop a reputation for being interesting are those who are genuinely interested in others. These people not only initiate spirited conversations; they listen actively and respond fully to their communication partners with probing and pertinent questions and statements. They also validate others as important in several nonverbal ways, including the use of direct eye contact, an alert body stance, and gestures that are both natural and appropriate to the topic under discussion.

Such vibrant communicators, by being consistently energetic and civil in both their verbal and nonverbal interactions, sustain meaningful conversations with all those around them. At the same time, they help their communication partners maintain equivalent civility and achieve greater self-confidence and self-respect.

One of the best ways to initiate productive conversations is to employ open-ended questions, as opposed to closed-ended questions. When you utilize open-ended questions, you obtain more engaging and in-depth responses from your communication partners.

Consider the number of times you might have asked people questions like these:

> "Do you like living in the United States?"
>
> "Were you pleased with the results of the midterm elections?"
>
> "Did you take part in yesterday's protest?"

"Have you thought about how the new tax law will affect you personally?"

All of these are closed-ended questions, and, if answered with a negative response, can abruptly end a conversation. On the other hand, if answered with a "yes" (and then followed by silence from the other person), these questions place a tedious responsibility on you to think of and direct even more questions to the other person. Kept at this pace, the conversation becomes more of an interrogation than a conversation, not to mention quite a drain on your mental capabilities!

Conversely, when you ask open-ended questions, you show a sincere interest in (and an added respect for) your communication partner. Open-ended questions favor increased civility and extended communication because they often begin with words and phrases, such as, *Why*, *How*, *What*, and *In what way(s)*.

Open-ended questions also add fluidity to your conversations and lengthens them because your communication partners can expand their responses beyond the words *yes* and *no*. Rather, your communication partners have the opportunities to provide responses and explanations that are thoughtful, thorough, and relevant.

Now, ask people you know only casually some of the following questions, and listen carefully to the answers given by your communication partners:

"Why do you think you would be successful as a state representative?"

"How would you describe the political climate in your region?"

"What was the turning point that led you to defend the death penalty in America?"

"In what way(s) could we best oversee the immigration challenges facing our country?"

"Why did you become a member of the Tea Party?"

"How do you respond to people who strongly advocate for more religious practices in public settings?"

"What qualities are most needed by any person serving as president of the United States of America?"

"In what way(s) does the American educational system need to be improved?"

"Why does there continue to be police officers involved in shooting (and often killing) unarmed black people?"

"How can we ensure that everyone in our country has access to affordable housing and healthcare?"

"What can we do—specifically—to help more able-bodied senior citizens find well-paying jobs?"

"In what way(s) should the criminal justice system be changed to ensure fairness for everyone?"

Especially in the heated atmosphere of contemporary politics can open-ended questions lead to remarkable civility between people. For example, to indicate you are honestly interested in another person's political views, you can initiate your discussion with an open-ended question.

This approach is particularly helpful when you're discussing politics with a person whose political philosophy is vastly different from yours. By asking an open-ended question right at the beginning of your conversation, you fully show your curiosity and interest in the person's ideas and values. Additionally, you demonstrate a genuine consideration and respect for the person's political beliefs though they may be radically contrary to yours.

Naturally, the answers to whatever open-ended question you ask will broaden the communication between you and your communication partner. With the details the person provides in responding to you, opportunities will quickly emerge for you to engage the person with more sincere questions or thoughtful responses that elaborate on what the person has just said.

Soon, you will be having a lively and pleasant exchange because both of you are learning new things about each other. In the process, each of you will eliminate the preconceptions you might have had about the other's political leanings.

Again, when you ask open-ended questions, you will receive more than a one-word answer and discover more about your communication partner's background, interests, and worldview. Equally important, you will validate your communication partner as an individual with unique personality traits, talents, and needs. Expressing such courtesy in all of your communication will give you the added advantage of being known as a "people person" who is very civil and honestly concerned about others.

Asking open-ended questions invigorates the life of any conversation and prompts both you and your communication partner to be more actively involved in the discussion. Using open-ended questions, in addition, helps you learn more about people and their experiences and viewpoints without being intrusive, manipulative, or obnoxious.

In political activities, such as press conferences, Town Hall meetings, panel discussions, and debate forums, open-ended questions can prove especially beneficial. They allow you to ask politicians and other public figures questions that require respondents to address issues in in a more descriptive and accurate way.

Far too often, particularly in public settings, we witness leaders or their spokespeople, not answering questions in a relevant, specific, or truthful manner. Despite intense pressure from their interviewers, these public figures seem unable to respond with answers that their audience finds clear and satisfactory. So, asking open-ended questions makes it difficult for people to reply with vague or evasive responses.

The many merits of using open-ended questions become even more evident when you are determined to elicit greater details and more explicit information from others in both private and public settings. In the end, open-ended questions supply quality and substance to a conversation and always sustain sound communication.

Try using these open-ended questions (and similar ones) to stimulate conversations with your family members, friends, and colleagues:

How did you learn about this new law?

What do you like best about being an American?

In what way(s) does today's political climate make you happy (sad, angry, nervous)?

How do your political views affect your relationships with your family and friends?

What is the best advice ever given to you by a political leader?

In what way(s) can United States of America make life more comfortable for marginalized people?

Never forget open-ended questions are the ultimate lifesavers in countless professional, personal, and social conversations! Not only do open-ended questions encourage your communication partner to provide more descriptive answers; they quickly improve your reputation as a polished conversationalist.

Small Talk That Pays Big Dividends

Small talk, like all successful speaking, requires you to develop excellent listening skills. The people who are best at small talk are those who listen best. Because they truly strive to understand and retain information provided by their communication partners, these individuals demonstrate a strong disposition and consideration for others. Is it any wonder these people are a joy to have at a social or business gathering!

No matter what you call conversations which are very social in nature—*small talk, chatting casually, gabbing, social discourse, yakking,* or *passing the time of day*—there is much information acquired by employing this type of communication. For example, you can gather many details from (and about) people when you speak with them in an informal setting. You can also develop an immediate rapport with them that may not be available when the conversation is heavily focused in only one area. You can further elevate your personal and professional status with your skill in making others feel important and relaxed while you learn what is truly meaningful to them.

The venerable and beloved actress Betty White provides timely information for all of us about being an effective communicator in her 2011 book, *If You Ask Me (And of*

*Course You Won't).*²² Ms. White discusses the value of genuine listening when one is a guest on a talk show (which you can apply to your own social interactions). In doing so, she reinforces the usefulness of listening to what others say to you.

> *"It goes back to that repartee and comedic timing both. You have to listen to people and play off what someone else says. You can't be thinking of what you're going to say next or it dies right there. If you listen to people, it triggers something in you to which you can respond. It's about both really listening and hearing that funny track that you can pick up and deliver back.*
>
> *"I can't tell you it's innate. I don't think it is. But I think you have a propensity for it. And after that, practice helps a lot."*

It is also crucial to keep in mind small talk conveys messages in a way that building blocks construct a house. Each piece of information you collect from a verbal or nonverbal source (regardless of how insignificant it *may* appear) adds to the whole message you receive during a conversation. These individual pieces or *clues* then indicate the best ways to respond to what you've heard. Often, you can learn just as much about the message from the speaker's facial expressions, eye contact, gestures, and other nonverbal indicators as you do from his or her words.

---

[22] White, Betty, 2011 *If You Ask Me (And of Course You Won't),* G. P. Putnam's Sons p. 137.

This attention on small talk is the result of the emphasis we place on well-developed social skills and civility at business luncheons, cocktail hours, and dinner parties. You may regard the content of the conversations as trivial and mundane, but the dynamics of both verbal and non-verbal interactions during these events could have a major influence upon your personal and professional success. Moreover, your gracious ability to engage in small talk can only add to your image as a person of great civility.

~~~~~

Your adeptness in using both open-ended questions and feedback techniques will doubtlessly help you achieve more productive and meaningful communication with others. Not only do these two techniques encourage your communication partner to provide added information to a conversation; they force you, as the listener, to pay stricter attention to the speaker's words and the emotional impact behind them. Both of these techniques have another advantage: they place importance on the speaker as a person with much to offer as well as a person worthy of your time and respect.

By enlisting these communication tips, you will rapidly learn people gravitate towards you because you display an authentic curiosity about the thoughts and opinions of others. You will further ingratiate yourself to others whenever you employ open-ended questions and feedback techniques during any highly charged political discussion because they reflect your sincerity in wanting to understand the speaker's position.

Clearly then, your civility towards people grows immensely as you widen your communication partners to include individuals who are distinctly different from you in education level, socioeconomic background, religion, race, or culture. Then, as you communicate with each person on a deeper and friendlier level, you will find you and your communication partner are more similar than you are different. This can only result in an enhanced understanding and respect for each other and insure a long-lasting civility between you.

So, no matter what personal or public occasion has caused you and your communication partner to be together, you can count on open-ended questions and feedback techniques to enliven and enrich any conversation you may share. Who knows where this will lead? You just may be surprised to discover how much you have in common with your communication partner.

Chapter 7
Your Oral Communication Speaks Volumes About Your Civility

You have been focusing on speaking and listening skills from the perspective of the receiver, the listener. Now, you are going to look at things from the other side—from that of the sender, the speaker.

What is speaking, anyway? Speaking is our most valuable tool for sharing ourselves with others. It's needed in all aspects of our personal and professional lives and is a major factor in how people perceive us.

Speaking is certainly more than just talking, conversing, communicating, or whatever else you refer to as *speech*. People with solid speaking skills say what they mean clearly, directly, and appropriately. They deliver their messages in a style and manner that is pleasant, courteous, and correct in grammar and diction.

So, it is your responsibility as a speaker—and sender of oral messages—to communicate with your listener as completely as you can. Then, you must ensure he or she accurately understands your intended message.

People with polished speaking skills pay particular attention to what they say and how they say it so their words always contribute to a productive, effective, and harmonious environment. Conscientious adults (and people in general) who strive to communicate in a positive way often achieve remarkable success in their lives and gain the respect of all those around them.

~~~~~

Simple things set the stage for outstanding speaking skills, such as your tone of voice. The distinct tone of your voice as a speaker (along with your positive filters, non-verbal signals, and your well-chosen words) helps you convey the message you wish to send to your listener.

Keep in mind words in and of themselves don't have much meaning. You, as a human being, give meaning to words. In fact, at least 30 percent of the interpretation of your message is dependent on your tone of voice alone.

It is usually your tone of voice that creates the initial impression someone has of you. As a result, *how* you say something often has as much to do with your personal and professional successes as *what* you say.

~~~~~

Talk isn't cheap. The emotional costs are exceedingly high in a country where low morale and low expectations exist because of a severely negative political climate. Such costs clearly lessen the efficiency, enthusiasm, and productivity of its citizens. When you express yourself poorly with words that are demeaning or insulting to others, you quickly (and, sometimes, unknowingly) breed tension, frustration, and anger in your immediate surroundings. Your behavior, not surprisingly, then contributes to an atmosphere that is depressing and divisive.

Imagine a professional colleague making this comment to you:

> *"I'm amazed you and Susan are able to get along well considering your inability to agree on most political issues."*

How does such a statement affect your attitude towards your work and towards your colleague?

It's wise to remember you build supportive relationships when you use words to affirm others and empathize with them. Your articulate use of positive terminology, in addition, reflects a heightened respect for your neighbors, friends, colleagues, and family members as unique personalities. In addition, your encouragement and validation allow the people in your life to grow emotionally and confidently on many levels.

Look at a revision of your colleague's earlier statement that is now more upbeat and understanding because of minor alterations.

> *"It's uncanny how well you and Susan get along because your political views are so different from each other."*

It is surely a much more effective and diplomatic statement than the earlier one.

We occasionally use negative words in confrontations with people, as well as in our descriptions of others, without ever examining the power of those words to devalue and discredit an individual. You must be extremely careful when you state explicitly—or even implicitly—that another person's political views, personal behavior, or ideas are not as significant or valuable as those of other people.

The words you choose in describing a person must also be accurate in meaning and affirming in spirit. Otherwise, you will only diminish the motivation of the person; attack his or her dignity as an individual; and help bring about an uncomfortable, unsettled, and disturbing social environment.

You are making an overly broad and crushing statement, for example, in describing someone as *incompetent*, *inadequate*, or *incapable*. By affixing the prefix *in* to these three words, you have removed every trace of the quality that could be associated with the person in your description.

You aren't saying the person is marginally competent, minimally adequate, or fairly capable. Instead, you are saying, plainly, the person does not possess *any* degree of competency, adequacy, or capability. It is the same with other words in your vocabulary that transmit a definite absence of a particular quality.

Consider the following situations in which the counterproductive words mentioned earlier are replaced with positive words to ensure ongoing and efficient communication between people:

Example   "Penelope, you are a totally *incompetent* press secretary."

Improvement	"Penelope, your skills as a press secretary could be further enhanced with more experienced people working with you."
Example	"The new research assistant demonstrated her *inadequate* grasp of the homeless situation in our state when she made her recommendations to the other committee aides."
Improvement	"The new research assistant's recommendations to the other committee aides indicates she must cultivate a better understanding of the homeless situation in our state."
Example	"Vic, are you *incapable* of even dialing a telephone to return constituent calls?"
Improvement	"Vic, I strongly believe you need to return telephone calls to constituents in a more expedient manner for both their benefit and ours."

According to several experts, people are more productive and enthusiastic in any environment where the emphasis is on complimenting a person's work and offering only constructive criticism when necessary. These experts also mention people within such a comfortable setting take less time to complete tasks reflecting quality and diligence.

With this in mind, you can frequently choose more favorable words to express your less than complimentary evaluations, opinions, and descriptions. In doing so, you maintain your own dignity by respecting the dignity of others. You also develop a more accepting and supportive community that motivates everyone (even those requiring much personal improvement) to increase the quantity and quality of their contributions.

On the contrary, if you use words to express blame, anger, and superiority, you just promote an even more hostile atmosphere and establish greater distance between you and your listeners. And you are definitely setting up a potentially volatile and counterproductive situation when you preface negative words with the accusatory "you."

For instance, you may say to someone in frustration, "You are so hopeless when it comes to handling deadlines." Or, in an extremely tense confrontation with another person, you might say, "You made me feel like a jerk!"

Again, words become positive or negative depending on how you, as a speaker, use them. It is especially important to remember you have the power—with your choice of vocabulary and tone of voice—to create an experience that is either rewarding or devastating for your listener.

~~~~~

As we have pointed out elsewhere in this book, there can be no compromise between people, groups, or political parties without a large focus on civility in their communication. So, when verbal disagreements escalate into loud and angry arguments, shouting matches, intentional insults, or bullying behavior, all hope for a reasonable dialogue or a thorough exchange of views disappears. The people who are part of these volatile situations, in all probability, will feel emotionally exhausted, unfairly treated, extremely irritated, or all three.

To prevent the growth of such dismal and depressing communication, you need to consider these five vital questions before you approach having any serious and meaningful discussion with others:

> *What specifically do I want to gain, take away, or learn from this exchange with my communication partner?*

> *What do I want my communication partner to remember or understand foremost from my verbal discourse?*

> *How can I maintain respect for my communication partner even when he or she is making it difficult for me to listen?*

> *At what point must I end my discussion with this person because he or she is demonstrating undue anger, disrespect, and hostility towards me or my colleagues?*

> *What positive and diplomatic words must I use to indicate I wish to continue a conversation at*

a later time with a person because it has become uncomfortable, unproductive, or uncivil for me?

You will improve your oral communication in any situation with your choice of positive words and appropriate tone of voice. In addition, these two factors can have a definite impact on how well your oral messages are received. Keep in mind the negative words listed in the second column, when employed with a negative tone of voice, can easily destroy your communication with another person. Consider the potency of the words in the list below and on page 133.

Words that can express positive feelings	Words that can express negative feelings
accepted	accused
appreciated	angry
authentic	condescending
capable	defensive
caring	discouraged
competent	dishonest
confident	dumb
devoted	failure
diplomatic	furious
encouraged	helpless
enjoy	hostile

genuine	hurt
gracious	guilty
happy	inadequate
honored	incapable
inspired	manipulated
invested	misrepresented
involved	patronized
pleased	powerless
proud	ridiculous
respected	stupid
rewarded	team player
team player	lie
trusted	undermined
valued	unfair

What You Think You Said May Not Be What Your Communication Partner Heard

Untold communication problems in both our personal and public interactions stem from confusion in semantics. Because different people attach different meanings to a particular word or symbol, messages are often full of ambiguity and uncertainty.

This naturally leads to major misunderstandings in professional and personal relationships. Consequently, individuals and organizations make decisions and take actions lacking fairness, specificity, and foresightedness. Are you a person who makes requests, issues directives, or provides analyses using vague terminology, such as *almost, soon, several, frequently,* and *somewhat*? Think about the confusion you may cause others when you communicate with ambiguous or nonspecific language.

For instance, what problems result for you and your communication partner when each of you has dissimilar interpretations of the italicized words in the previous paragraph? Which of these words would be defined in the *same* way by you *and* the other person? Most important, how does mutual understanding between the two of you enrich your communication and build confidence in each of you?

Unless your communication partners are aware of the meaning you attach to your words—or you are incredibly lucky—you may be placing yourself in awkward, if not dangerous, positions whenever you rely on vague terminology.

~~~~~

To the people who use profanity-laden language, we say its time you enlarge your vocabulary. Even if those close to you are not offended by your coarse language, your limited vocabulary speaks volumes about your lack of self-respect and consideration for others.

Let's start with a common reason for employing coarse or vulgar language: Everyone speaks like that these days! So, following that logic, we who don't find such language intellectually stimulating, nor even conversationally compelling, should avoid bars, baseball games, and other public gatherings because we will be language outliers.

The second problem with the frequent use of profanity is its degradation of the English language. It's amazing we would want to express ourselves so poorly with a beautiful language that comes so naturally to us when millions of people throughout the world struggle to learn and employ English in myriad business, education, and social settings.

We spend so much of our education learning to communicate well in English it seems like constant swearing (dirty language, colorful speech, profanity, or whatever you choose to call it) is a *dumbing down* of our language. It also seems like a rejection of all the quality effort we (and those who taught us to communicate both correctly and elegantly) spent as children and young adults to be articulate, expressive, and, most of all, understood and more engaged with the world in which we live.

When you think about the emotions involved in using profanity, you invariably realize there are often angry components tied to obscene words. For example, a person usually swears spontaneously when in an agitated state. Because the person is feeling angry, frustrated, annoyed, or sometimes livid, he or she blurts out words without thinking about their meanings or relationships to a particular message or situation.

You learned earlier your tone of voice usually has a profound effect on someone's initial impression of you. People also form impressions of you based on how well you use the English language. Grammatically careless speech can be potentially damaging to you as a speaker because it may demonstrate an inadequate educational background, lack of professional competency, limited social skills, or little self-confidence.

People from divergent backgrounds and socioeconomic levels strive daily to eliminate poor grammar from their social and workplace interactions. These ambitious individuals very much want to reflect refined and competent language skills. Indeed, skilled and motivated professionals everywhere know Standard American English is *still the* model for both oral and written communication in American culture, education, and business.

Get a Grip on Your Grammar—As You Get a Grip on Your Speaking!

Though it's always important to use correct grammar, there are certain grammatical goofs that attract the attention of— and annoy— many people. Here is a list of grammar goofs found in writing and speaking over the years that participants in Corporate Classrooms' workshops have mentioned as their pet peeves. Avoid these mistakes so the "Grammar Police" will never question you:

- Inserting *like* at the beginning of a sentence when there isn't a comparison made. For example, "Like my girlfriend, she gets mad." *Like* can be effectively used to compare people and things in addition to acting as a verb. Thus, a proper comparison using *like* is, "Lucy is just like her father in temperament."

- Misusing the words, *continuous* and *continual*. A leak in your bathroom that won't stop is *continuous*. Your despair at returning to your office on Monday morning may place you in a *continual* state of anxiety.

- Overusing the word *bottom line*, both in speech and writing, when other synonyms would be fresher and more original. Why not try *most important* or *pressing concern, foremost matter*, or *primary aspect* instead of *bottom line*? After all, the bottom line—oops—your most important concern in language skills must be communicating your thoughts in the most effective way.

- Using *goes* for *said*, as in "Then, he goes to me, 'You're nuts!'"

- Beginning a sentence with *anyways*. Anyway, *anyways* is not a proper word, and it is never correct in a sentence.

- Saying *Febuary* for *February*, *libary* for *library*, and *expresso* for *espresso*. Additionally, when you say *ehtihkwet* instead of *etiquette*, *tenative* instead of *tentative*, or *recanize* instead of *recognize*, it is clear you need to polish your oral communication skills

- Using the phrase "To tell you the truth..." as a preface to any statement is redundant unless you intend to tell a lie to your listener.

What Is Speaking Anyway? It's Far More Than Your Voice

- Using *uninterested* when you really mean *disinterested*. *Uninterested* should be used when referring to a person who does not care, is indifferent, or is bored. *Disinterested* is correctly used to describe a person who is objective and unbiased about something. "Many people are *uninterested* in watching television shows that depict violence. Nevertheless, there are thousands of people who are *disinterested* critics of television programming for children."

- Employing sloppy diction as *Dijyaeet? No, ju?*

- Answering the phone in a grammatically incorrect way. For instance, if you were to respond affirmatively to the question, "Is this Bill?" the correct response would be, "This is he." Or, if your name is Bella and you wish to respond positively to a similar inquiry, then the correct response is, "This is she." On the other hand, assuming you are Bill or Bella, the response, "Yes," would be just fine, too.

~~~~~

The following words below and on pages 139 and 140 are frequently mispronounced by many people. The surest way to use correct pronunciation is to refer to a current dictionary whenever you are in doubt about the sounding of a word. Practice this list and your own tongue tanglers as well!

abdomen	hearth
abominable	height
acclimate	hospitable
applicable	idea
architect	impotent
athlete	inclement
bludgeon	inculcate
braggadocio	inquiry
chic	irreparable
comparable	irrevocable
congratulations	harassing
corps	incredulity
coup	immunology
coup d'état	Italian
coupon	laboratory
creek	library
data	lingerie
de rigueur	maintenance
despicable	mischievous
docile	obnoxious
encore	often
espresso	otolaryngology
etiquette	picture
exacerbate	placate

exasperate	placid
exegesis	plethora
execrable	pumpkin
exponential	recognize
exquisite	reunions
extraordinary	sandwich
familial	skewered
February	sword
fecund	supposed
finance	tedious
finite	temperament
formidable	tentative
gape	terrorists
gesticulate	texts
government	thrash
grimace	thwart
gubernatorial	tourists

At the beginning of this chapter, we posed the question: What is speaking anyway? Chapter 7 has demonstrated that speaking is much more than just talking.

Speaking is one of the most immediate ways we connect to one another as human beings. It is not only a medium for expressing our thoughts and ideas with words. Equally important, speaking is one of the most expedient ways we have to communicate our emotions and feelings with our voice, in terms of its tone, pitch, rate, volume, and articulation.

Furthermore, your most frequently used communication instrument is often your voice. Like all instruments, it requires careful cultivation and protection. Your constant attention, throughout your life, to enriching and refining this exceptional instrument will reward you with greater success in developing your personal and professional relationships; expressing both your concrete and abstract ideas; and sharing your deepest feelings, emotions, and passions with those you most trust and appreciate.

Speaking, too, is the most common method you employ in reaching out to others in a highly technological society. Just think of how many people in the United States alone use cell phones, smart phones, Skype, social media, live streaming videos, and online meeting applications! Keep in mind, modern technology has allowed you the luxury of face to face communication even when you are not with others in person. As a result, you can now see and converse with people who are thousands of miles away from you.

Consequently, so much of what you share with people in a single day—for example, fair and accurate news; detailed knowledge of intellectual topics; colorful descriptions of ongoing events; up-to-date information about the weather; new language skills; and a rapport with your colleagues and family members—are dependent on your ability to speak well with others and use your voices in the most constructive fashion possible.

You rely on your speaking ability in a multitude of other ways to express yourself to people with whom you interact every day. As you do, these same people receive an impression of you. So, to guarantee you leave all of your communication partners with a positive feeling, be certain you always speak with them with clarity, civility, and empathy no matter who they are or what they represent.

Your voice, more often than not, will be the key that connects you emotionally and intellectually with people in public or in personal surroundings. Above all, it is your speaking ability that will make a unique and permanent impact on others.

Chapter 8
Empathy and Assertiveness: The Bookends of Civility

Empathy and assertiveness are two human behaviors often discussed and debated when considering the divisiveness in America today. But a large number of people lack a deep understanding about these two types of behavior. Amazingly, people continue to confuse empathy with sympathy and assertiveness with aggressiveness. They then behave accordingly which, in turn, reinforces their confusion about the concepts and behaviors related to empathy and assertiveness.

Simply stated, *empathy* is your attempt to understand another person's feelings—the source of which may be anger, sadness, frustration, commitment, enthusiasm, or any other human emotion. *Assertiveness*, on the other hand, is your ability to express your personal feelings and thoughts confidently to another person without intimidating, threatening, or coercing that person. Furthermore, you will enhance the quality of your assertiveness when it is accompanied by your genuine empathy.

What then is the powerful connection between these two behaviors? It is that each behavior strengthens and refines your sharp focus on civility. Equally important, it is the positive use of the pronoun *I* to demonstrate true civility in expressing your empathy or assertiveness in any given personal or public setting.

Combined with a proper tone of voice and choice of words, the word *I* frequently creates a climate in which a meaningful exchange takes place between two people. Additionally, using the pronoun *I* immediately establishes (albeit subtly) the objective and flow of the conversation because it propels the speaker into the role of producer. With his or her use of *I*, the speaker highly influences the mood, content, and end results of the conversation.

Employing the word *I* is evidently not comfortable for a vast number of adults. Perhaps they were expected as children not to use *I* more than once or twice in a conversation. These adults were apparently taught that using *I* conveys conceit, aggression, or self-centeredness. However, if you as a civil person wish to develop greater empathy and assertiveness, then you must become comfortable utilizing the word *I* in your daily interactions with others.

You will become more comfortable applying the word *I* in your speech when you shed *three* myths surrounding the use of *I*:

> First, by adopting the word *I* to express your understanding and self-assurance, you are not being tactless or overbearing.

> Second, by exercising the word *I*, you are not acting in a self-centered or conceited manner.

> Third, by prefacing your statements to others with *I*, you are not necessarily provoking a confrontation, even during a heated exchange of words.

It's always wise to remember *I* statements help you to personalize your communication because you take responsibility for your feelings, ideas, and expectations while expressing them succinctly and directly. This responsibility is based on the premise your feelings, your ideas, and your expectations *belong to you*. Therefore, you have a right to express yourself as long as you don't threaten or hurt others in the process.

Instead of saying,

> "We admire politicians who put their principles before their political party."

You can personalize your communication further by using *I*.

> "I sincerely admire politicians who put their principles before their political party."

Instead of saying,

> "So many people I know dislike political arguments."

You can state assertively,

> "I, for one, dislike political arguments."

Also, *I* statements actively involve you, the speaker, as you communicate with other people. By using *I* statements to express your thoughts, you avoid mistakes caused by ambivalent, confusing, or passive communication.

Instead of saying

> "A group of us think we need to be more direct with the President about his unseemly behavior."

You can be very direct and declare,

> "It's clear I need to be more direct with the President about his unseemly behavior."

Instead of saying,

> "All of us caused the confusion by revealing only the noncontroversial parts of the recent Congressional bill to the press."

You can simply and honestly utter,

> "I alone caused the confusion by revealing only the noncontroversial parts of the recent Congressional bill to the press."

Furthermore, *I* statements are valuable because they do not threaten your listeners nor discredit you as a speaker. You clearly are being empathetic or assertive—or both—when you use *I* statements. As such, you confidently and accurately convey your feelings, ideas, and expectations without attacking or accusing your communication partners.

Instead of asking,

> "How can you put up with the Speaker's inaccurate comments about your Chief of Staff?"

Say,

> "I find it very difficult to listen to the Speaker's inaccurate comments about your Chief of Staff."

Instead of saying,

> "Congressman, with all due respect, you spend way too much time worrying about your popularity in your district."

Say,

> "Congressman, with all due respect as a fellow member of Congress, I worry more about doing the most good for the most people in my district rather than how popular I am with my constituents."

Several phrases you use every day reflect the positive aspects of *I* statements because, with these phrases, you hold yourself accountable for your remarks, opinions, and feelings:

- "I am..."
- "I want..."
- "I must..."
- "I need..."
- "I feel..."
- "I am sorry..."
- "I expect..."

All of these are all suitable prefaces to statements that express your personal feelings.

Now, look at how these same words are used to express your empathy and assertiveness depending on your specific communication situation.

Accepting Another Person's Feelings (Empathy)

I agree with you about the need to be more open about our findings.

How can I help you? I want to support you and your party in every way I can.

I am sorry. I was out of line when I made a sarcastic remark this morning about your mother serving in our Administration.

I can easily see why you would feel angry about the lack of objective news coverage related to your investigation.

I'm sad things are so difficult for you right now as a freshman Senator.

I am certain my staff and I will be able to expedite the documents your family needs to transfer your daughter to a hospital in Germany.

I plan to do all I can as your Congressional Representative to locate your husband who is missing in China.

Expressing Your Feelings (Assertiveness)

I am extremely disappointed in the way you spoke to the parents of the deceased veteran.

I must reiterate the high ethical standards required in your new position at the Federal Bureau of Investigation.

I plan to share this information with the Department of Justice immediately.

I expect everyone in this office to remain calm and focused in spite of today's tragedy.

I need you to be more respectful towards my colleagues when they express their opinions.

I feel you don't appreciate all the time I have spent helping you and your family.

I want to be very clear about our expectations for the midterm elections.

For a few moments, assume you are a member of the White House staff who speaks to one of your assistants about a project that needs completion before Friday:

"You should have this project completed by noon on Friday. Otherwise, some people will end up working at the White House over the weekend, and they will not be happy with you."

In this situation, there is a huge possibility the listener could misinterpret your words. He or she may think you *wish* to have the project completed by noon on Friday, but you will also understand if it isn't. In addition, your listener could be wondering to whom you are referring when you use the words "some people."

A revision of your statement incorporating the word *I*, nevertheless, leaves no doubt about the meaning of your words in the listener's mind:

"I need to have this project completed by noon on Friday. Otherwise, I will end up working at the White House over the weekend, and that will not make me a happy camper."

With such wording, you have clearly and concisely stated your needs, expectations, and feelings about the project under discussion without intimidating your listener. Your staff member fully understands you want him or her to finish the project by noon on Friday, and *you* will be unhappy if you have to work at the White House over the weekend to complete the project. It is evident you are speaking only on *your* behalf. Also, with your statement, you are being specific and taking personal responsibility for your words.

Again, *I* statements cause you to personalize your communication, be actively involved in the communication process, and avoid threatening your listeners. *I* statements will also serve you well when you wish to express your thoughts and be accountable for them without upsetting or annoying your communication partner.

Consequently, *I* statements help you to be both assertive and empathetic in your personal and professional life. These statements will assist you in remembering easily and accurately what you say to others. Such assertions will ensure your communication partners receive your messages willingly and correctly.

So, the next time you're feeling concerned, compassionate, frustrated, or annoyed, try using an *I* statement to express your point of view in either an empathetic or assertive way. You'll be pleasantly surprised at how this form of self-expression deflects tension; gains you the respect of your friends and colleagues; and helps you take control of any potentially demanding situation.

~~~~~

Especially in America's current political climate, we need to apply the strength found in *I* statements whenever we are engaged in an earnest political discussion. Remember the importance of discussing any political topic with others is the exchange of ideas, facts, and personal anecdotes related to the topic.

In this way, we not only reveal our opinions and feelings to others so they understand the source of our convictions; we also learn about the opinions and feelings of these people that, in turn, help us comprehend and empathize with their positions.

Using *I* statements is always a healthy way to maintain a lively, respectful, and informative conversation with your communication partner no matter how deeply each of you cares about your viewpoint. As we pointed out earlier, you can convey an empathetic or assertive tone with your *I* statements. Either approach will serve you well as you maintain a positive, upbeat conversation with whomever you discuss a sensitive or controversial issue.

Jovani: *Some of our group want to attend the rally to protest arresting asylum seekers without a trial. Would you want to go with us, Anita?*

Anita: *Absolutely not. It would be an affront to my values and beliefs. Let these people go somewhere else. As it is, they've taken jobs away from my family, my friends, and my neighbors. Why should we let these criminals from all these countries into our country? I worked hard to get where I am today. I didn't get food stamps or welfare or free health insurance. I work*

> to put food on the table for my family. I work so my family has health insurance.

Jovani: I understand how you might feel pushed aside, Anita.

Anita: Pushed aside! No one pushes me or my family to the side, especially illegal immigrants.

Jovani: I know you feel strongly about this issue, Anita. Because you do, I think you might be interested in knowing about my family. My father entered this country twenty years ago as part of an asylum program.

> Before he arrived in the United States from Lebanon, he had survived two attempts on his life by separate groups and feared for his life most of the time. If he were arrested at the border, without a hearing and sent back to Lebanon, he would be dead today.

> I am also proud to tell you my father finished his engineering degree here. Then, he met my mother and started a family. He's now CEO of a major company in our city and is a major contributor to its arts and cultural programs.

Anita: Your father wasn't a criminal. His background is different than all the others from South America and Mexico and I respect that fact.

Jovani: *I know you're entitled to your own opinion, and I respect that. I do, however, hope we can agree a judge should decide if the asylum seekers are criminals before returning them to their native countries. Nonetheless, I believe there is a great likelihood, if these immigrants are deported, they will be murdered or jailed when they return to their former country.*

Undoubtedly, you can utilize the word *I* on so many levels to express both your genuine empathy and diplomatic assertiveness as you interact with others. Whether it's a personal matter in which you are comforting a friend in distress; a work situation that requires compliance with guidelines you have established; or a social event that calls for your intercession to settle a dispute between two entities, your sophisticated use of *I* can be a powerful communication tool for you.

Your insertion of the pronoun *I* will be a significant help to you when you wish to reduce the tension in a delicate or highly emotional situation. This approach naturally requires a suitable and ingratiating tone of voice as you convey *I* in such an encounter. Consequently, you will avoid unpleasant outcomes and resolve potential conflicts with—or between—others whenever you use I in this way.

People frequently hesitate to use *I* at the beginning of their statements or comments because they fear the word reflects a conceit, bravado, or false confidence. On the contrary, your ease with using *I* shows others you are a take charge person with a healthy sense of self based on responsibility, confidence, and a sincere desire to deflect (or minimize) animosity anywhere.

Some people have an uncanny ability to ascertain the mindset of each person embroiled in a conflict. These same people quickly grasp the key issues or feelings inherent in the conflicted individuals. So, when these skilled communicators use *I,* they swiftly bring peace and order to any potential confrontation, no matter the situation.

For example, a group of your friends (composed of both males and females) are having cocktails at a nice restaurant before sitting down to dinner. Then, one person makes a comment about one of your friends' sisters which upsets the sister's brother very much. In a few moments, everyone is shouting and taking sides as the two friends are about to assault each other physically.

Fortunately, one person in the group has a keen talent for resolving tense moments and restoring order to a potentially volatile situation. He immediately says to the assembled group, "*I* want to ask all of you a question. Why are we doing this? We've all known each other for years and know each other's values so well. So, let's face it! The comment was not meant to hurt anyone. *I* know each of you very well, and I know you care deeply about each other. So, *I* suggest we all try to relax before we go into the dining room to have dinner together just like the old days!"

The lesson these people teach us is the importance of getting involved in both challenging and unpleasant situations if we definitely want to create a more civil and sane society. By their fine example, these exceptional communicators remind us that standing on the sidelines, waiting for someone else to intervene, or hoping that a resolution will suddenly appear out of nowhere is futile. This means, of course, we can only restore civility in our own lives by assuming responsibility and striving to change adverse situations into cohesive and harmonious moments.

This is an exceedingly difficult challenge for anyone, even for a person with outstanding communication talent. Let's be honest: the restoration of civility takes courage— the courage to act, the courage to face angry people, the courage to use our intuition, and, most of all, the courage to live out our values rather than just proclaim them!

In the end, putting the power of the *I* pronoun to its best use will teach you new lessons about confidence you never knew you had. While you build ever stronger communication skills with the use of the pronoun *I*, you will also be helping America find its way back to a more thoughtful, refined, and civilized nation.

And *You* Can Do a Lot for You, Too!

In Chapter 6, "Feedback Techniques and Open-Ended Questions: Vital Keys for Connecting with Others," we discussed ways to help you be a more active listener. We also demonstrated how you can use the pronoun *you* effectively to let your communication partner know you are definitely following his or her messages.

By simply using the word *you* to paraphrase the words and feelings of your communication partner, you show the other person you fully comprehend the thoughts and emotions he or she has just conveyed to you. The use of the pronoun *you* in this manner is very appropriate because it does not sound threatening nor blaming.

Obviously, your listener will enthusiastically accept any of these sentences:

> "You gave an outstanding speech in Congress yesterday!"
>
> "You have never disappointed me as my campaign fundraiser."
>
> "You were so convincing on the news program when you discussed your reasons for the new Aid Bill."
>
> "You have no idea how much you have helped our subcommittee this session."
>
> "You continue to be a delightful and efficient office administrator!"
>
> "You have that rare quality of making everyone feel welcome and important."
>
> "You will undoubtedly be very successful in broadcast journalism."

All of the previous statements beginning with *you* cannot be misinterpreted when expressed with a positive and gracious tone of voice. So, as you begin a sentence with *you*, be certain it is followed by a statement that will elevate, inspire, flatter, or otherwise make your listener receptive and eager to receive your message.

Here's Where *You* Takes a Wrong Turn!

On the other hand, there are many other situations when using the pronoun *you* in your speaking can be highly inflammatory with its accusatory, judgmental, and condescending manner. Introducing sentences with *you*, while using a negative or counterproductive tone of voice, creates a difficult communication experience that could have long-lasting effects for both you and your listener.

Consider how you would react if someone addressed you with any of these comments:

"You can be a real jerk at times."

"You must be joking, right, that you plan to be the first female of color to represent our district in Congress?

"You don't know what a server is?"

"You can't afford to be in this gubernatorial campaign."

"You don't seriously think you'll get the White House appointment?"

"You have lied to your constituents so many times it's incredible!"

"You really are delirious if you believe a woman can be President of the Unites States in this environment."

It isn't hard to realize, as you review the previous sentences, you could easily alienate all of the people to whom you direct such remarks. Moreover, the use of *you* in each of these statements only serves to heighten its extremely unfavorable tone.

This style of communication demonstrates your arrogance as well as your need to find fault with others. It also shows your inability to foresee how using harsh and demeaning language—in just one sentence—can ruin your relationship with another person.

~~~~~

It's clear to see that our everyday language—even small pronouns used in speaking, such as *I* and *you*—have immense power to change the tone and direction of a conversation. To be an outstanding communicator, then, you must not only be aware of the proper use of personal pronouns; you must also be sensitive to the emotional strength of these words.

Chapter 9
Avoiding Roadblocks That Prevent Successful Communication

In our modern, everchanging language the term *information network* is not limited to computer usage. In business, as well as in your personal life, you are part of a large information network. During family discussions or conversations with other loved ones, you express very personal thoughts and feelings.

When you are about to make a purchase, you ask various questions about that purchase. In your day-to-day business conversations, too, you constantly exchange information with coworkers and clients. The success of all of these communication situations is related to how clearly you speak and how accurately you listen to your communication partners.

Meanwhile, do you ever start a conversation with someone, and then realize, after only a few moments, you are not communicating effectively with the person? If this does happen to you, do you also take the time and effort to analyze why the interaction between you and your communication partner is dissolving? Usually, when looking for a reason why communication breaks down between you and other people, you may discover you set up a roadblock that marred the exchange!

You create a roadblock each time you communicate in a negative way, verbally or nonverbally, with another person. Naturally, this severely limits your communication partner's understanding of your message and prevents any further meaningful conversation between the two of you.

It is almost impossible to share your ideas or information with someone with whom you are not truly communicating. Furthermore, you cannot easily gain the support, compliance, or cooperation of a person you have placed in a verbal or emotional maze.

Speaking and listening are the starting points—and can be the stopping points—of much communication. Key elements in the information process are lost when you aren't fully listening, understanding, or acknowledging your communication partner and his or her situation. The lost information then leads to a breakdown in a relationship and often leads to many hurt feelings and missed opportunities.

All of us, at one time or another, are capable of placing verbal and emotional barriers in front of people with whom we are attempting to trade information. As a result, these barriers dictate how well our communication partners listen to us and how well they respond to us.

Communication Roadblocks That Create Gridlock

Listed on the next several pages are potential communication roadblocks that face every speaker. Examine each roadblock carefully. The warnings and wisdom pertinent to each roadblock will help you avoid the pitfalls of different communication roadblocks and become a more sophisticated speaker.

Abusive Language

In addition to being unsophisticated and unprofessional, the use of obscene or demoralizing language usually is indicative of the low self-esteem of the person who uses it—not to mention the person's extremely limited vocabulary.

Abusive language is just that because it makes many listeners feel uncomfortable, threatened, or invalidated. Consequently, it is never employed by a person who truly wishes to demonstrate courtesy and communicate effectively with other people.

> *Author's Note: We believe it best for you to provide your own example!*

Accusations

Whenever you direct an accusation at someone, you run the risk of backing that person into the proverbial corner in which the person will react defensively and distrust you and your motives.

Accusations, often grounded in arrogant and volatile power plays, have an insidious way of destroying prime opportunities for communication between people. Because all accusations reflect blame, they instinctively place people in a *we versus they* situation.

Is it any wonder then we automatically lose people's trust, respect, and cooperation when we accuse them of misdeeds? Once the *blame button* appears, the accused party or parties tragically (yet understandably) waste valuable time defending themselves or rationalizing their behavior. The accusers, meanwhile, are heavily responsible for the air of hostility and frustration that now prevents any productive communication between them and those they have accused.

> *"What do you mean your IQ is higher than mine! No one has a higher IQ than me. Do you hear me, Brampton? No one has a higher IQ than me. And don't you forget it!"*

Arguing

This particular roadblock not only inhibits communication between you and your communication partner; it lowers the morale of all those around you whether at home, at work, or in public. The sheer essence of arguing—negative in tone and defeatist in attitude—only results in an immediate environment that is unsettling, uncomfortable, and nonproductive for all concerned.

Whenever you sense a discussion between you and another person is escalating into an argument, it is time for you to conclude your remarks and take a break. You will, otherwise, enter a new verbal territory full of innuendoes, suspicions, and tensions. An argument based on documented and relevant facts is the only acceptable form of argument.

> *"I don't believe you, Dreyfuss! My base would never make comments about me like the ones you mentioned!"*

Blaming

When you begin conversations with phrases, such as, "You didn't do...." or "You weren't..." you immediately place your communication partner on the defensive. Too, the people you place on the defensive will behave in one of two ways. They will talk their way out of a situation and shed responsibility for their actions. Or they will emotionally *shut down* and not listen to anything else that you may say.

Blaming others (even if you feel justified in doing so) is the antithesis of mutual rapport because it always leads to negative feelings and poor understanding between people. It is critically important then for all of us to replace potentially blaming statements with language that affirms—and not threatens—another person's sense of well-being.

> *"Barry, the Congresswoman wanted those notes before her meeting with the committee. How could you not place a priority on the Congresswoman's orders? You'll be the cause of her downfall, Barry! Mark my words!"*

Criticism

"You can catch more flies with honey than with vinegar" is an adage that aptly applies to the communication process because criticism without a constructive or kind purpose often acts like a verbal clubbing. So, don't expect true cooperation or respect from someone whom you have beaten into submission by your harsh words and comments.

If, however, you first take the time to compliment or praise someone, that person will be more accepting of any *constructive* criticism you may offer at a later date.

> *"You really are a ghastly Chief of Staff. You can't even fire someone without leaking it to the press."*

Discounting

"Uh huh," "sure," "whatever...." Whenever you respond to someone's comments with these and similar words, you transmit the message he or she has said nothing of real consequence or value. In rankings of communication patterns that bother people, this behavior is often at the top of the list—or near the top!

So, why then should your communication partner, who could be your opponent by this time, continue a conversation with you? When you discount others, you are not even giving them the respect and validation that are the heart of all sound communication.

> *"Oh sure, Marge. I'm certain my constituents will just love attending the rally in the middle of a cow pasture."*

Dishonesty

Your credibility in communication is much harder to maintain once you have proven to others you are not trustworthy. There can be no cooperation without trust between colleagues or between loved ones, and, without cooperation, there can be no agreement or unity.

In addition, the domino theory, in which one situation affects another, takes over whenever there is an absence of compassion and honesty in the interactions among people in any individual setting.

> *"Ana, I respect your desire to be honest. But, just once, I would appreciate you slightly inflating the polling numbers we release to the press about my popularity with constituents."*

Distractions

If you allow your distractions to complicate the communication process, you are, in fact, telling the person to whom you are speaking he or she is not worth your full attention. You further demonstrate three unflattering traits of your personality when you allow distractions in your mind: your lack of focus; your inability to organize your thoughts; and your disregard for others' time and worth.

Therefore, how you manage distractions speaks volumes about you as a person—and as a listener!

> *"I know you won't mind me interrupting our national security meeting so I can give a quick interview to Box News. It's particularly important my constituents hear the real news about who's behind the sinkhole discovered on the Capital grounds."*

Emotional Outbursts

When you become extremely emotional during a discussion, you confuse the issue and add instability to the situation. Always stick to the subject, and don't burden your communication partner with any emotional problems you may be currently facing.

You have a definite responsibility to your communication partner to be as clear and focused as you can be in conveying your message. By injecting comments and a tone of voice that reflect self-absorption and self-pity, you digress from the topic at hand and create further distance between you and your communication partner.

> *"It's all fake news! I just want you to know how stupid Congressman Housefire was to run me into the ground. I have been a loyal supporter of the Congressman for seven years, and he just overlooked me as a possible replacement for his Congressional Aide!"*

Ethnic Slurs

Using ethnic slurs exposes boorish, ignorant, and perilous behavior. Likewise, the person who utters ethnic slurs within a workplace or other public realm deceptively destroys morale and cooperation.

Quite simply, ethnic slurs should not be tolerated in *any* form. Instead, ethnic slurs must be recognized for what they are: a precursor to dangerous stereotypes and a deliberate distortion of facts in any work environment.

> *"Those colored people are ruining this country with all of their minority-status nonsense."*

Hidden Agendas

Using this technique as you communicate with others is equivalent to taking advantage of someone. You're exploiting their openness with you. You are also fostering dishonesty whenever you maintain hidden agendas. Dishonesty, in any form, contributes significantly to a weakening of camaraderie and strength in any relationship.

A cohesive personal or professional relationship cannot last long wherever dishonesty exists. The very nature of hidden agendas (manipulation, deceit, and secrecy) virtually assures hurt feelings and lack of trust will abound in any relationship. In addition, your reputation among your friends and associates suffers immeasurably each time you communicate with a hidden agenda.

> *"I know we have been considering Jane Parra for the Congressional Committee spokesperson, but I just received the resume of Clyde Wilder, a friend of mine, who has much more experience. I think we should put Jane on hold until you can talk to Clyde."*

Interruptions

If you are not willing to give your communication partner your undivided attention, what message are you conveying to that person? Be sure to schedule a sufficient amount of uninterrupted time to converse with others.

Each interruption means a particular conversation will take longer and will result in a waste of valuable time. Unfortunately, interruptions occur all too frequently in our daily lives today. It appears there are very few people who recognize the critical importance of making each moment count and focusing on one specific activity or discussion at a time.

> *"As I was saying, Raquel, before Deputy Secretary Quigley walked in.... Oh, hello Representative Grassroot! How was your vacation? I'm sure you won't mind waiting just a second, Raquel. I need to speak with Representative Grassroot about something important."*

Intimidation

People usually react to this technique by shutting down emotionally. No matter what your message of intimidation is, it often translates into a version of, "If you don't do what I say, I'll do something unpleasant to you." Such intimidation naturally causes the people who are in a defensive position to place enormous emotional distance between themselves and their accusers (aka *intimidators*).

Moreover, all personal or professional bonds are damaged because they no longer reflect fairness, consideration, and respect. The connection, if any remains, instead reflects rigidity and pressure—unmistakable evidence of a tense and uncomfortable association. The process of intimidation, left unchecked, eventually permeates all of your encounters and leads to a *complete breakdown* in communication.

> *"If you don't have that backstabber, Congresswoman Beauregard, on the phone within ten minutes, I will fire you on the spot!"*

Jargon

The communication between two people is apt to suffer whenever one of these people uses jargon that is not clearly understood by the other. You must be exceedingly careful to use jargon (words common to a specific field or profession) only to *enhance* communication, not embellish it with an air of authority.

Is your listener as well-versed in a particular subject as you are? If not, your use of jargon can be as confusing to him or her as if it were an unfamiliar language. Keep in mind successful people strive to *express* themselves clearly, and not to *impress* others, while communicating with colleagues and clients in and out of today's workplace.

> "The generals have decided they will deploy unmanned aerial vehicles for aerial reconnaissance missions prior to engaging in air combat maneuvering. The unit will also guide the use of airborne forces employing remote long-range electronic surveillance systems located in safe zone regions."

Jumping to Conclusions

Slow down! Mistakes impede progress. Get all the facts, study them, and lay out a strategy. Remember, an army never won a battle by using the "Ready. . . fire. . . aim" method. Keep in mind apologizing to others for your mistakes takes time—time that could have been much better used to improve the level of quality and harmony in all of your relationships.

> "You mean you never returned General. Tallchief's call, Thomas?"
>
> "I tried to reach her, but she wasn't available. So, I left a message with her assistant."
>
> "Oh, you left a message with her assistant. Well, that's better, Thomas."

Manipulation

Manipulation, an extremely cruel form of dishonesty, is a detour that never rejoins the main road. The act of manipulation is always concerned with demonstrating who has the most control.

So, this type of conduct slowly extinguishes all spontaneity and flexibility that normally abound when people trust and respect each other's judgment. Manipulative behavior, in time, fosters an unhealthy atmosphere in relationships that breed fear, insincerity, and demoralization.

Any relationship in which one person manipulates another is certain to end poorly, if not disastrously.

> *"If you structure the voter survey the way I suggest, Vera, perhaps I'll be able to act on your request for vacation time more quickly."*

Negative Attitudes

It is exceedingly frustrating to interact with people who possess a negative attitude. With such an attitude, these individuals not only minimize their own opportunities for success; they place major obstacles in front of others who believe anything is possible when one works hard to obtain it.

In a way, people with a negative outlook have allowed their poor self-image to determine the quality and quantity of their life experiences. Remember there was "The Little Engine That Could," *not* "The Little Engine That Couldn't." Say "I can," and you are halfway to your goal! Say "I can't," and you have sealed your unfortunate fate.

> *"I will never get all of this work done! I can't complete these constituent calls in the time Senator Emilio has allocated for me to finish!*

Nonstop Talking

How can you expect a person to respond if you talk incessantly? How can someone feel free to speak openly while you dominate the conversation? Don't think of the person with whom you're speaking as your verbal opponent or as someone who has to be assaulted with words.

Nonstop talking indicates many unflattering aspects of a person's personality, not the least of which is his or her self-centeredness. Most of all, one who engages in nonstop talking clearly does not understand that genuine communication must actively involve all communication partners, not just the ones who can utter the most words.

> *"As I was saying, Ms. Clements, I think we need to look at that idea of yours again in about three months. I was saying to Secretary Brightwood you are quite a thinker when it comes to these brilliant ideas. It's too bad other young women, like you, don't take more of an initiative. I think that's what's wrong with the political world today—that and too few women who actually act on their brilliant ideas."*

Not Having Feelings Validated

To ensure communication is productive, effective, and ongoing, the feelings of your communication partner must be validated. Your attentiveness, gestures, and eye contact are just a few of the many ways in which you validate your communication partner.

Your empathy and responsiveness throughout a conversation are two more ways to validate the other person. When you disregard another person's ideas, comments, or opinions, you invalidate the individual's worth and integrity. You are, in a sense, flipping the *off switch* to a person's emotional comfort zone by not affirming his or her words. More than any other element, the act of validation assures your communication partners you respect them as well as their time, consideration, and effort.

> *"Do you really think it's necessary to take the time to discuss your blatantly erroneous hypothesis, Major General?"*

Patronizing

Each time you patronize or talk down to someone, you are being condescending and insensitive. You are, in effect, saying to the person you possess more knowledge about a particular topic than he or she does. Your ability to communicate positively *is* now invalid!

Don't ever give into the temptation to provide additional explanations or descriptions to another person just because you think the person needs such details. Always *ask* someone if further information is necessary. Otherwise, you run the risk of appearing boorish and arrogant to colleagues, friends, and even strangers.

> *"You place the mouse cursor, the object that looks like an arrow, over the big, red "Confidential" button on the lower-left corner of the display screen and push the left mouse button only once. Remember, Assistant Deputy Secretary Meyers, only once. Sometimes, you click the left mouse button twice. This time, it's only once. Then...."*

Preaching

This communication barrier is similar to the previous one in that it easily reflects the arrogance and insensitivity of the speaker. Those who preach to others soon find their congregation, as it were, diminishes rapidly! Most individuals quickly tire of preaching by friends, relatives, and coworkers simply because such sermonizing reflects unequal treatment of others. Bear in mind, too, those who *preach* force their opinions and values upon an unwilling and uninterested audience.

The whole purpose of reaching out to others is to create *more* solid communication. So, unless you have an organ and a willing flock, it is best you leave the preaching to those in the clergy.

> *"It is exceedingly important to all the country, Marcus, that you always bring to light the very conservative viewpoint when dealing with the posts on our website. And, believe me, knowing you are promoting the views of many conservative Americans will make you feel so much better, Marcus. You do understand me, don't you, Marcus?*

Rejections

The person who sees possibility in everything knows the immense value of respecting *all* ideas and the *people* behind those ideas. On the other hand, one who quickly rejects someone's ideas conveys an opposite—and negative—message: both the idea and the person behind the idea are unimportant.

In your workplace, and in your personal life, it is wise to remember your rapid dismissal of a person's idea or comment cuts to the heart of his or her identity. Your rejection, in effect, says loudly and clearly, "You and your contribution are not very important." How then can the person making the contribution feel empowered enough to continue talking with you?

> *"You can't be serious, Nadene! No one in this country will ever agree to separate children from their parents even if they are crossing the*

border illegally! What made you think of that idea?"

Sexist Remarks

Sexist remarks create monumental roadblocks to sound and respectful communication whether they are obvious or subtle in nature. These remarks are potentially lethal in destroying any constructive communication that may occur in any arena in today's rapidly changing world.

Sexism of any sort is destructive for all of us because it is based on both a lack of reality and a lack of fairness. Furthermore, sexist behavior in the contemporary workplace, aside from being inappropriate and offensive, is often illegal. And it can—and frequently does—prompt litigation.

> "Let's be real about this! This year is just not the time to consider a woman as president of the United States of America."

Shoulds and Oughts

Be careful how you use the words *should* and *ought*. Gentle suggestions and encouragement will earn you more productive rewards than a holier-than-thou attitude. Stating it another way, people will usually resent you for telling them what they should or ought to do when they haven't asked you for your help or advice.

People far too often invalidate the feelings of friends, family members, and colleagues by telling them what they should or ought to do. Furthermore, those giving unsolicited advice many times predicate their opinions on *their own* experiences—and not on the experiences of the people with whom they are speaking. Remember you are on decidedly shaky ground whenever you offer *unsolicited* advice to others by suggesting what they should and ought to do.

> *"Gretchen, you should stand up to Admiral Higgins when he makes you stay late to finish researching his political positions. You ought to tell him you need to pick up your four little kids."*

A Final Word About Communication Roadblocks

When confronted with inappropriate or offensive behavior, don't respond with similar behavior. If you do so, you only stoop to a lower level.

Always consider the source of inappropriate or offensive behavior. It helps you immeasurably in understanding why getting upset is counterproductive.

Make certain all of your criticism is constructive. If *any* of your criticism is said to hurt, demean, or shock someone, don't offer it.

If you need to speak to someone firmly or to discuss a delicate matter, be sure to do so in an area away from other people.

Remember people have a right to their opinions and feelings whether you think their opinions and feelings are important or valid.

Never expect a person to do work you would not do yourself.

Be careful not to invade someone's personal boundaries. You violate both their privacy and dignity when you do so.

Avoid prefacing statements with the word *you* when disagreeing with someone. It minimizes the accusatory or confrontational tone of the disagreement.

Eliminate as many distractions as possible when you're communicating with another person. Not to do so is a major violation of social etiquette.

Consistently say, "Thank you," "Please," and "Hello" to your friends, family members, and coworkers. You'll be amazed at how contagious this polite behavior is in creating a warm and hospitable environment wherever you are.

Compliment those around you when they have done something well, productive, or kind. When people know you are prone to accentuate the positive, they will accept your constructive criticism more easily.

Treat everyone as your equal, and you will be treated as the equal of everyone else.

Ask yourself if you would take the advice you are about to give to another person.

Don't take yourself too seriously. Keep in mind a healthy sense of humor derives from genuine humility.

~~~~~

Undoubtedly, successful people are those people who are respected by others. These successful people get their respect the old-fashioned way: they earn it by respecting themselves and everyone else.

Chapter 10
The Top Ten Talking Turnoffs: The Quickest Way to Alienate Others

People, unknowingly, in both their personal and professional life, often use a style of speaking that creates uncomfortable, hostile, and adverse conditions. Simply by their tone of voice and choice of words, these people alienate their communication partners (whether an individual or a group) and encourage incivility for everyone involved.

There are several *styles* of unfavorable speaking listed on the next seven pages that may very well prevent others from responding to you in positive and productive ways. Among these are ten distinct patterns that are all too prevalent in the world-at-large today. These ten patterns are recognized as the source of much frustration and counterproductive behavior in personal, professional, and public settings throughout the country.

Each of these speaking styles is dangerous because it is based on judgmental attitudes, inflexibility, and a refusal to treat people as individuals with unique talents, needs, and personalities. Furthermore, some negative speaking styles are subtler than others in their damage because they appear in the guise of passive or nonconfrontational communication.

Take time to analyze the factors in the following examples that contribute to a negative speaking style. Then, review the suitable and assertive response to each speaking style for better ways to manage a similar communication challenge in the future.

1. Ordering, directing, commanding, pulling rank

    The person who employs this style obviously thinks the militaristic approach brings the best—and most efficient—results to solving any problem or overcoming any challenge. Additionally, this person is prone to interject the pronoun *you* with his or her imperialistic remarks.

    Talking Turnoff

    > "I'm have been the Congressman for this district for over twenty years. So, you cannot tell me what's best for my constituents!"

    Suitable Response

    > "Well, Sir, I am not only one of your constituents, but I have lived in this district longer than you have. So, I believe I have a promising idea, too, about the needs of the people in this district. And, Mr. Congressman, I would like to remind you that your constituents elected you to serve them and honor their wishes—not the other way around."

2. Warning, threatening, intimidating

People who demonstrate this style, somehow, have a challenging time understanding human beings do not respond well or productively when they are backed into corners. Nonetheless, those who attempt to manipulate people with warnings, threats, or intimidation do so for fear of losing power or prestige whenever others exercise their freedom or individuality.

Talking Turnoff

> *"I'm ending this discussion if you don't stop criticizing our President."*

Suitable Response

> *"First of all, I thought we were discussing the strengths and areas for improvement of the President. Secondly, I want us to have a better understanding of each other's political viewpoints. So, I'd like to share with you a few strengths I do see about our President."*

3. Lecturing, patronizing

This style of oral communication states volumes about the speaker's true feelings, not the least of which is his or her offensive generalities or assumptions about other people. Underlying all the speaker's words is a presumptuousness that reflects both arrogance and condescension.

Talking Turnoff

> *"I'm only trying to do what's best for you, Elaine."*

Suitable Response

> *"I appreciate your concern about me. However, like you, I'm an adult with a variety of experiences that have made me very resourceful. So, I'm sure I can resolve this issue all by myself."*

4. ## Practicing pop psychology

    The pop psychologist has a reason or theory for any emotion expressed by a colleague or friend. Consequently, the pop psychologist often overlooks the reality of another person's situation. The need of the pop psychologist to convey a psychological reason for everything most often creates ambiguities and confusion for his or her listeners.

    Talking Turnoff

    > *"Of course, you aren't cooperative because you felt left out of the planning."*

    Suitable Response

    > *"Actually, I am trying to cooperate, but I'm having a tough time voicing my opinions while so many people are talking over one another and raising their voices.*

5. ## Interrogating, accusing, shaming

    Succinctly stated, the person who practices this behavior firmly believes the key to motivating other people is through good old-fashioned humiliation and blame. This person, in other words, has adopted a certain strategy for coping with whomever he or she engages at work, at home, or in any other environment. The adage "The best defense is a good offense" clearly describes the person's communication philosophy.

Talking Turnoff

> *"Why wouldn't you be in favor of a zero-tolerance immigration policy for our country? You have to be realistic about the effects this policy would have on people already living in the United States."*

Suitable Response

> *"I have several reasons and facts to share with you about my disagreement with the zero-tolerance immigration policy. Before I share this information with you, I want to remind you that I consider myself not only a very realistic person, but also a person who is well-informed about the many effects of this policy."*

6. Injecting sarcastic, stereotypical, or labeling remarks

One who displays this speaking style naturally interprets the world—and those in it—in terms of an *us versus them* philosophy. This person further believes the height of professional eloquence is the quick and demeaning retort.

Talking Turnoff

> *"Of course, there's more minority people in American jails. They commit most of the crime."*

Suitable Response

> *"Really? That's strange. I just read an article that contains many relevant statistics about this problem. And this article also states there is a disproportionate number of minority people in US jails. Furthermore, the authors cited both current and relevant facts provided by the United States government."*

7. Withdrawing before reaching a resolution

People who resort to this speaking style demonstrate infantile and immature behavior. Storming out of a meeting, abruptly ending a conversation, and clamming up are visible symptoms of these individuals who need to be coaxed to do something and be recognized for their compliant behavior.

Talking Turnoff

> *"Just forget it. You apparently don't care about my views on the LGBTQ community!"*

Suitable Response

> *"I'm sorry you feel that way because I certainly do want to hear your views on those who identify as LGBTQ. I'm also interested in hearing your opinions about this community particularly because you told me earlier you have two uncles who are gay.*

8. **Demonstrating narcissistic or highly self-absorbed behavior**

It's exceedingly difficult to engage in conversations with narcissists because they always want the focus on themselves and are categorically concerned with their own needs and desires. Also, narcissists rarely admit to making mistakes or offer apologies for hurting others' feelings or causing social upheaval. Unsurprisingly, narcissists consistently emphasize how an action, event, or comment has affected *them* and have little empathy for others' misfortunes.

Narcissists are frequently objects of scorn because they have spent so much of their lives indulging themselves and their wants. Equally sad, narcissists hardly ever experience the deep emotions of understanding and compassion that unite most human beings.

Talking Turnoff

> *"I'm the most successful business person ever. Nobody's ever been more successful in business than me. And I know how to run a government, too."*

Suitable Response

> *"Everyone knows you're a successful business person, Sir. I'm especially interested in understanding just how your vast experience in the business world would translate to being a leader of an entire country."*

9. Speaking in a dishonest or misleading manner

The person who employs this speaking style could spend hours discussing the difference between a *little lie* and a *big lie* or between *fake news* and *factual news*. Nevertheless, in most work and personal relationships, this person eagerly avoids honesty and accuracy in oral communication.

Dealing openly with others (especially those in authority) is often threatening to this person because he or she fears taking individual responsibility for ideas and actions. Unfortunately, for all those involved this person sees only unfavorable outcomes whenever truth and accountability are part of productive discussions and activity.

Talking Turnoff

> *"It's clear that most people receiving government aid refuse to work."*

Suitable Response

> *"Wow! That's quite a statement. I learned not long ago that most people receiving food stamps in the US are either children or senior citizens. Obviously, many of these people cannot work. Nonetheless, I am aware there are many, many seniors who have all been turned down for jobs recently. They were all well-qualified and physically able to do the jobs, too."*

10. Peppering speech with vocal pauses, colloquialisms, and poor grammar

People who depend on vocal pauses, colloquialisms, and poor grammar clearly do not understand the importance of sound language skills and their effect on their personal and professional reputation.

These individuals reveal a lack of sophistication and confidence by using awkward phrasing, inappropriate terminology, and incorrect grammar. Over time, the same people, with their deficient language skills, may negate any personal and professional stature they otherwise have earned and enjoyed.

Talking Turnoff

> *"I, like, never understood, like, um, your hang-up about, um, religion."*

Suitable Response

> *"I'll be as clear as I can about this. I have a strong religious belief—a hang-up, as you would say—because I love the sense of community my religion provides and the guidelines it offers for living a life of service to others."*

And, Yes, You Are Responsible for Others' Feelings

The thoughts of the well-known author, poet, and playwright Maya Angelou have been quoted innumerable times because of their profound insight. The following quotation from Ms. Angelou not only provides a valuable lesson about the effect we have on others during our lifetime; it is a genuine reminder of what we actually leave behind us after we are gone.

> *I've learned that people will forget what you said, people will forget what you did, but people will never forget how you made them feel.*
>
> —Maya Angelou, American' Poet

If ever there was an observation to guide you in face to face communication and improving your civility towards others, this quotation by Maya Angelou must be one of the wisest and most practical! Just think of all the people you have met in your life (and there are a tremendous number of people you can't even remember). Yet, it's easy to recall the individuals who have truly made you *feel* worthy, special, unique, happy, or respected. They could be a parent, teacher, friend, roommate, sibling, boss, coworker, or neighbor who has never failed to treat you as an honorable and exceptional person.

You can recollect many details about your experiences with such a person because he or she was so positive and uplifting for you. In short, this individual made your life not only memorable, but meaningful. Moreover, this person has clearly left an indelible mark on your life because of his or her deep concern for you; strong belief in your singular strengths; and recognition of you as someone who would always make a difference to others.

Unfortunately, there are also those in your life who have left you with an unfavorable or indifferent impression because they did not treat you well or even kindly. Unlike your memories of people who have motivated you, these people will serve as negative memories and stand out in your mind because their words and actions made you feel small, unimportant, and unappreciated.

So, the words of Maya Angelou will continue to have significance for you as you interact, in both your personal and professional life, with people who have distinct personalities. You should also recognize the words and actions you use in conveying your feelings to other people have immense power to inspire or demean them. Equally important, you must not forget the feelings you leave with others may be their sole—or lasting—impression of you.

You create worthwhile exchanges with others when you speak with a positive tone of voice and choose diplomatic words to express your thoughts. And, by employing genuine civility in all of your messages, you build communication that consistently leads to beneficial outcomes.

Chapter 11
Using the Tremendous Power of Nonverbal Communication

You communicate with *positive* body language whenever your nonverbal communicators help you express, emphasize, or enhance your communication skills as a speaker or listener. No matter what communication role you play, positive body language stimulates and heightens communication between you and your communication partners.

There are thousands of nonverbal communicators. Nonetheless, most of these signals fall into four areas: eye contact, facial expressions, gestures, and posture.

Many people, in most aspects of their lives, pay little attention to these nonverbal behaviors. These same people may not realize every part of their body language—whether small or large—adds or detracts from the power of their messages.

In fact, according to numerous social scientists, approximately sixty percent of a person's message is expressed in his or her body language. (That figure jumps to approximately ninety percent whenever tone of voice is included in nonverbal communication!) To improve your civility, it's imperative you monitor your own body language to ensure it not only mirrors your exact messages, but it also displays your sincerity, passion, and depth of feeling.

The expression, "a picture is worth a thousand words" is particularly relevant to polished communication skills. If you have ever tried to discuss something of importance with someone who slouches in a chair, constantly shifts, checks the clock, or yawns, you know nonverbal communication can be deafening. You can certainly say a great deal with just your hands, your posture, or one lifted eyebrow!

Also, consider people who have their arms crossed tightly over their chests while their mouths are closed and pursed. Or think about people who respond to a question with several vocal pauses (such as ahh, umm, or mmm...) with a facial expression that can only be described as one of a deer caught in a car's headlights. What message is being sent by people who disagree with your point of view (but evade saying so directly) while their eyes are close together as they speak to you with a smirk? If your judgments are on verbal pause, then put them on physical pause, too. Your body records your emotional state and clearly telegraphs any message you care—or don't care—to send.

To understand fully the impact of your nonverbal behavior on others, you must first reflect upon how other people might interpret your nonverbal signals. Keep in mind you use *acquired* gestures unconsciously, but they mean different things to different people. The interpretation of any nonverbal behavior is often based on the observer's culture, religion, politics, economics, geography, values, and so forth. There are, to be sure, many interpretations of any nonverbal movement you make.

Whether you are the speaker or listener, you must use nonverbal communication that directly and forcefully emphasizes your messages. Otherwise, your communication partners will not perceive your thoughts accurately. Nor will these people understand the deep emotion and essential meaning of your communication. Don't ever forget your nonverbal communication is also a common measuring stick for others to evaluate the honesty, intensity, and extent of your messages.

If you doubt for a moment the power of nonverbal communication, consider how shallow, unexciting, and inaccurate your verbal descriptions would be with either inappropriate or nonexistent body language. No matter where you look—in business, politics, medicine, or elsewhere—nonverbal communication is at the heart of every message conveyed or received, whether in a face to face encounter or conversations over the telephone.

Conversely, it is extremely hard to engage your body language in a productive way when your attitude is a negative, blaming, or unpleasant one. You simply sabotage your nonverbal communication with others because of your inner tension, anger, or intolerance. The adage "attitude is everything" remains true and relevant in all parts of our life.

It is, therefore, vitally important for you to maintain a body language that reflects a positive mindset so you can find success in both your personal and professional life.

Equally important, you must demonstrate a body language that all of your communication partners clearly understand. With such attentiveness, your nonverbal communication will endow you with a still greater reputation as a skilled communicator.

While you speak and listen to others, they gather an immense amount of information from your eye contact, facial expressions, posture, hand gestures, and body movements. These hundreds, if not thousands, of nonverbal signals tell your communication partners just how involved you are, or want to be, in communicating with them.

As noted earlier, approximately 60% of all human communication is nonverbal in nature. Do you think nonverbal communication in today's world is highly overrated? If so, you may need to review the following statistics, and determine their influence on your day-to-day communication:

- Human beings are capable of using 700,000 nonverbal signals with accompanying messages based on studies by noted linguist, Mario Pei.

- In other research conducted by Ray Birdwhistell, a well-known kineticist, it was proven human beings are capable of using 250,000 facial expressions with distinct meanings.

- Human beings are also able to demonstrate 5,000 hand gestures with associated messages. This fact was established by M. H. Krout, a prolific kineticist, during his study of nonverbal signals made with hand movements.

- Similarly, G. W. Hewes, another famous kineticist and anthropologist, recorded that human beings are skillful in using 1,000 postures to express a particular idea or feeling. Mr. Hewes discovered this phenomenon while conducting research on people's postures and their numerous meanings.

Nonverbal communication can be used very effectively even when speaking directly to people via telephone or by other electronic means. Though you are not physically with a person (or a large group of people), you can often establish a sense of face to face communication with your tone of voice and nonverbal communication. Obviously, the more animated your voice and nonverbal behavior are, the more powerful your message will be.

You can exhibit solid body language even when you cannot see a person's face. You can, for example, exude relaxation, confidence, and warmth in any situation with forceful, yet proper, nonverbal communication. Additionally, by standing or sitting erectly, extending your arms, raising your eyebrows, or nodding your head, your messages are conveyed more succinctly and dynamically as you speak to others whom you cannot see.

For an illustrious example of outstanding communication with others over the telephone, just think about the "Fireside Chats" that Franklin Delano Roosevelt[23] implemented early in the Great Depression (and in his first administration). President Roosevelt won over millions of Americans, both Republicans and Democrats, with his warm and conversational speaking style during these

---

[23] Thirty-second President of the United States of America from 1933 to 1945.

weekly "Fireside Chats." Furthermore, while he was president, Franklin Roosevelt transmitted his "Fireside Chats" over thirty times using a fairly innovative device, the radio.

As Hazel Rowley, the author of *Franklin and Eleanor: An Extraordinary Marriage* (copyright 2010) said so beautifully about the magnetism President Roosevelt demonstrated in these chats:

> *Secretary of Labor Frances Perkins would attend all of the thirty-one fireside chats FDR gave during the twelve years of his presidency, and she never failed to be moved. "His mind was focused on the people listening at the other end. As he talked his head would nod and his hands would move in simple, natural, comfortable gestures. His face would smile and light up as though he were actually sitting on the front porch or in the parlor with them. People felt this, and it bound them to him in affection."*
>
> *With his first fireside chat, Roosevelt achieved what seemed almost impossible. He persuaded people to take their money back to the banks. He explained, simply but without condescension, why he and his advisers had decided to close the nation's banks and reopen them gradually, and he appealed to the people to play their part. "I can assure you, my friends, that it is safer to keep your money in a reopened bank than it is to keep it under the mattress... We have provided the machinery to restore our financial system; it is up to you to support it and make it work. It is your problem no less than it is mine. Together we cannot fail."*

> *Better than any politician in his time, Roosevelt understood that the new art of radio was about informality. He managed to convey the impression that he was chatting with a neighbor by the fire, while beside him his mother sipped tea and Eleanor knitted.[24]*

~~~~~

It might surprise you to know the one nonverbal activity understood by all people throughout the world and that easily connects them as human beings is smiling. Smiling is the most recognized nonverbal signal on earth to indicate a human being's pleasure, happiness, or satisfaction. Furthermore, a smile has extraordinary power to deflect volatile situations, improve customer service, increase sales, strengthen teamwork, and convey hospitality in today's business world. Because smiling requires so little effort, few people consider how important this nonverbal signal is in their day-to-day personal and professional activities!

As a result, the act of smiling is sorely lacking in all aspects of our society. Millions of people every day exchange money, deliver products, order new inventory, and solve myriad problems, all in the name of customer relations. Yet, they conduct all of these activities without ever displaying the one symbol that *clearly* indicates satisfaction with a product, process, person, or result. How much stronger their messages of appreciation would be with a broad smile!

---

[24] Rowley, Hazel *Franklin, and Eleanor: An Extraordinary Marriage, Franklin and Eleanor: An Extraordinary Marriage,* Farrar, Straus and Giroux, Copyright 2010

Think about the numerous times you've walked out of a store or an office and thought, "What a dud!" (or had some similar reaction) when recalling the person with whom you had just interacted. Upon closer examination, you realized you felt this way because the person had been so impersonal and never flashed a smile, even when thanking you, expressing gratitude for your patronage, or complimenting you and your company.

Eye Contact

Your eyes express a number of nonverbal messages that strengthen both your verbal and aural communication. In many ways, your eyes are your first step in establishing a bond with your communication partner because they signify your interest in the person and your respect for his or her individuality.

Eye contact further helps you keep your mind on the message at hand, and it involves you in the emotional and factual content of what is under discussion. Additionally, eye contact encourages you, whether you are speaking or listening, to look directly at your communication partner.

Your eye contact reflects your self-confidence and many of your other valuable personality traits. Also, it expresses several emotional elements that are part of your personality at any given time. Emotions, like surprise, warmth, sadness, joy, disappointment, respect, curiosity, and pride are some of these.

Always look at the person with whom you are communicating. This is not stating the obvious when one considers how often people say to their communication partners (be it coworkers, acquaintances, spouses, or children), "Would you please look at me while I'm speaking to you?" In reality, the more you concentrate on the speaker, the less chance there is of you misunderstanding the message—and less chance of the speaker misunderstanding your reaction to his or her message.

It is equally important, as you strive to improve the quality of your eye contact, not to dwell on a person's unique facial or bodily features nor to look away from any person who is speaking directly to you. Get in the habit of looking directly at a person's eyes. Remember, though direct eye contact demonstrates rude behavior in some cultures, it is highly prized and admired in all areas of American culture.

Facial Expressions

Facial expressions are an important part of your nonverbal communication. Your facial expressions provide several clues for your communication partner. In Western culture, particularly, people who are very animated in their expressions and movements are well-regarded and respected. This is because animated people, with their nonverbal communication, often prevent us from becoming easily bored or inattentive. The body language of these lively individuals simply adds visual appeal to their communication. These people, with their vigorous body language, announce to everyone, "I am actively involved in the conversation; I care deeply about the subject;" and "I definitely want my thoughts and feelings understood by others."

Facial expressions can send many powerful messages. They can demonstrate your respect for others; reflect your interest in someone or something; indicate your curiosity in different subjects; show your enthusiasm for life; transmit your positive attitude about people, places, and ideas; convey your ambition as a working professional; express your compassion for your coworkers, family, and friends; and serve as a *sneak preview* of the dynamic individual behind your face.

Gestures

These are the movements you make with various body parts, especially your hands and arms, to add emphasis to your messages. All gestures—to be effective—must be appropriate for your purpose and natural to *your* style.

Inappropriate and awkward gestures, such as the following, may detract from your messages and alienate you from your communication partners: pointing at people; touching others to emphasize an idea; being too familiar (for example, putting your arm around a person whom you do not know very well); invading people's personal space; displaying obscenities with your fingers; hands, and other body parts; and holding someone's hand longer than a few seconds during a handshake.

Posture

Naturalness is, once again, an asset in exposing body language that is positive and genuine. Always stand erect and walk with your shoulders back and stomach in so people will easily recognize your self-confidence, awareness, and enthusiasm. On the contrary, you often exhibit a lack of self-confidence and a poor self-image whenever you engage in the following nonverbal behaviors: hunching your shoulders; slouching in a chair; leaning forward with your head or chin resting on one of your hands; sitting on your hands; and shifting your position constantly while standing or sitting.

You, as a speaker or listener, also need to be careful about yawning, stretching your muscles, or leaning your arm or body against a wall. These behaviors may be interpreted by some of your communication partners as a lack of interest in them and their feelings.

Also, you would be wise to avoid the following nonverbal behaviors that may indicate your timidness or lack of purpose: walking stiffly, walking hesitantly, or walking with your head down as if you are looking for something on the ground. Let your arms swing back and forth as you move along. By doing so, you emit naturalness, relaxation, and self-confidence. Be deliberate with your footsteps, and people will perceive you as a determined and purposeful individual.

~~~~~

Today's political events throughout the globe places unique boundaries on common communication strategies. Knowing how to handle your eye contact, gestures, and even the common handshake can make a difference in your ability to communicate your messages in various parts of the world.

Nonverbal communication is a key element in how you are perceived by others during your interaction with them. The adage "It's not what you say, but how you say it" is particularly apt for people who travel throughout the globe. In many regions of the globe, it is especially important you convey a positive image of yourself through your nonverbal communication.

You should also know as much as you can about the customs and ceremonies of people in other cultures with whom you are (or will be) communicating. Such preparation will enhance all of your body language for more productive communication with people from these cultures.

Learning a foreign language is easy when compared with improving your body language. Most languages are organized with specific rules of grammar to facilitate writing and speaking. In fact, many languages are rooted in an alphabet or group of symbols that provide the language with a distinct identity. Thus, you can verbally communicate your thoughts easily to people who speak a particular language, once you've mastered its grammar and vocabulary.

Conversely, your success in relating nonverbally to those of another culture depends on how well you communicate with your body. It is imperative then you learn the nuances of all nonverbal signals in a particular culture to interact successfully with natives of that culture. Naturally, the more familiar you are with a culture's "silent language," the better your chances are of not committing obvious—and, sometimes, offensive—violations of etiquette in that region of the world.

Global diversity is no more evident than in the nonverbal communication used by various cultural groups to transmit the essence of their messages. On the surface, many facial expressions, body movements, and gestures appear to be exactly the same. The meaning, however, of each action in any particular culture has the power to carry a strong singular message. The message could be one of happiness, respect, or insult! Of course, the impact of any gesture's message is dependent upon the understanding of the person who receives it.

In the United States, for example, forming the thumb and index finger into the letter *O* is indicative of wholehearted approval. It is the American way of saying something is "A, okay." Nonetheless, you shouldn't ever use this same hand gesture when dealing with a native German as well as people in Mediterranean, South American, and Middle Eastern countries. This specific gesture is extremely vulgar and disrespectful to German residents (and those residents in countries mentioned above) because it symbolizes the human anus.

~~~~~

Information networks link what were once the most inaccessible places on earth, and global travel can be accomplished in a matter of hours. Unless you want to appear as unsophisticated or unknowledgeable, you must remain mindful of cultural differences in nonverbal communication wherever you are.

Interacting electronically with others or traveling throughout the world also requires your attention to the most minute aspects of body language. It is your responsibility as a citizen of the world to verify, study, and recognize the subtle behaviors each culture uses in communicating with other people.

Despite the recent rise of nationalism in some countries, it is helpful to remember the mixture of ideas, resources, and corporations in several countries has made nationalism a secondary concern. This places a greater responsibility on you to understand the cultural differences existing between groups of people as you strive to promote a positive image of the United States of America throughout the world.

The keys to any successful business or political negotiation in any global setting are a deep respect and a large tolerance for cultural diversity. Without these, your productivity and effectiveness (not to mention your image and that of the people and country you represent) will certainly be affected in an adverse way.

Sometimes, even when you believe your intentions are honorable and you will be understood, you discover very quickly just how wrong you are! This is not a matter of political correctness where labels change with the prevailing social and political movements. Often, body language, gestures, and other forms of nonverbal communication are governed by history, heritage, customs, and, of course, religious beliefs in a certain area.

You must make a huge effort to communicate a precise message with nonverbal signals. To disregard this advice is to ignore the dignity of the people with whom you are interacting. Furthermore, to neglect such guidance is not only inappropriate; it is dangerous because you run the risk of transmitting an incorrect or improper message and insulting your international colleagues.

How then do you communicate most effectively in a nonverbal manner with people in any part of the world? It is critical you prepare for your meetings with natives of diverse cultures by absorbing as much information as you can concerning their customs and practices. Elicit the help of those who have experience with such societies or who have had firsthand experience with the mores of a certain region. Embassies, consuls, tourist boards, and libraries are also great sources of help in gathering the information you need.

Your resourcefulness and persistence in obtaining material about the beliefs, customs, and values of these cultures will pay tremendous dividends to you as a global traveler and representative of the United States. Your international neighbors will absolutely appreciate your respect and knowledge of their cultures. As an act of gratitude, they will open their doors of communication even wider for you!

~~~~~

Bodily movements and facial expressions are additional tip-offs to others about what's really on your mind. Nonverbal signals, depending on how they are transmitted, reveal many different messages. Therefore, reading the signals of body language is an important part of interpersonal communication.

If you ever want to see the dynamics of nonverbal communication in action, go to a busy post office in an American city. Observe the unspoken messages that are conveyed by each person waiting in line to be serviced by a postal clerk.

As one customer moves ahead, the next person may or may not move. Why does this happen? Also, why do some people only move inches ahead when the people in front of them have moved several feet ahead? The answer may be found in the perceptions of body contact held by these customers. They may well regard quick movement that results in being close to another person as an aggressive or rude act.

For many people, stepping too close to another person is rude because it is an invasion of the person's space—the invisible area around a human being that is sacred to him or her. This private area is shared only with others (close friends, family members, romantic partners, and so forth) on a personal or an intimate level. So, if you casually enter a person's private space, you may disrupt his or her sense of security and comfort as well as injure the person's dignity.

~~~~~

The eyes, poetically speaking, are the windows of the soul. In some cultures, you must peer through "these windows." For instance, inhabitants of most desert regions, such as Saudi Arabia, consider direct eye contact as very manly behavior. It is, therefore, a sign of great disrespect and weakness *not* to make strong eye contact if you are a man.

Native people in numerous Asian countries, on the other hand, make direct eye contact with others only *briefly*. It is also considered a sign of rudeness to make direct eye contact with an elder within these countries.

If you were to sit with your eyes closed during an average American meeting, other Americans would assume you either did not sleep enough the night before or you were bored. Interestingly, if you displayed the same behavior during a meeting in Japan, it would be regarded as perfectly acceptable by all meeting participants. Your colleagues would understand you were concentrating intensely on the current discussion and were paying particularly close attention to each word uttered by the speaker.

~~~~~

Hands are used for different purposes in diverse cultures. For example, in Middle Eastern countries, men are often physically affectionate with each other. They frequently embrace and hold the hands of the man with whom they are communicating. However, it is inappropriate for a woman in this part of the world to have any physical contact with a man who is a stranger to her.

In Japan, too, hand contact is much different between people than in the United States. A simple head bow is customary practice and a way of greeting another person in much the same way as the handshake is used in the United States. Nonetheless, many Japanese, especially those in younger generations, are adopting the custom of shaking hands as is often found in Western culture.

The exchange of a business card is another culturally distinct behavior. Americans, for example, will give their business cards to other people and expect recipients of those cards to unceremoniously glance at them, and then deposit the business cards into a pocket, card case, or briefcase.

Using Japan again as an illustration, the business card in Japanese culture is regarded as an extension of one's self. The Japanese use both hands, as in presenting a precious gift, to deliver their business cards to others. The person who receives the business card reads it thoroughly while holding it with both hands. The card is then moved to a place of honor by the recipient. With this in mind, the card is never used as notepaper because such an action would insult the person from whom it was received.

Though most people have two hands, the hands of each person are, without question, not equal in many cultures. In the Middle East, to cite one prime example, the left hand is considered the unclean hand, and it is used only to perform bodily functions. Obviously, it is never used to touch food or to greet another person.

~~~~~

Careful! In the United States, people nod their heads in an up and down manner to show they are in agreement. Additionally, they move their heads in a right-to-left fashion to say "No." These are not universally accepted signals, however. In some countries, the behavior normally interpreted by Americans as "Yes" is often interpreted by natives as a resounding "NO!" So, it's important for you to understand the facial expressions of the residents of any country you plan to visit or in which you plan to work.

Consider, too, people in some countries, such as Argentina and Peru, tap their heads with their forefingers to denote they are thinking. The same action applied near the temple of one's ear, by people in other places indicates, "This is very clever." In many other countries, this behavior may be translated as either, "That's very intelligent" or "He (or she) is crazy." People in Holland, meanwhile, tap the center of their foreheads to clearly suggest, "He (or she) is stupid" or "That's crazy."

The act of whistling, too, holds different meanings in diverse cultures. Americans whistle while they work to show they are in a good mood or to express their approval or to praise others. Or Americans might whistle to demonstrate their boredom with an activity. Conversely, people in Great Britain look upon whistling as a form of jeering and do not regard it as a friendly and respectful gesture.

~~~~

Americans involved in politics, business, international relations, military affairs, and tourism are exceedingly conscious of the messages expressed by excellent posture. A man or woman exhibiting exceptional posture in the United States is readily identified as a person with a healthy amount of self-confidence, poise, and determination. Indeed, a person sitting or standing erect sends a strong signal to others that he or she is alert and eager to be productive.

Most working adults in America, nevertheless, are apt to view people sitting in a slouching or lounging fashion as not being attentive or professional. How you carry yourself, as described by a majority of successful professionals, is a solid indicator of the message you are about to deliver!

Though it may be a pun, even your feet carry a great deal of weight as a nonverbal communicator in several regions of the world. The Middle East is one of those regions. So, it is an insult to expose the sole of your foot to people in this area as they believe the feet to be the lowest and dirtiest part of the human body.

Think about what would happen if you placed your feet on a desk or crossed your legs at the knees in the Middle

East the way people frequently do in the United States! It is wise to remember Americans' informal behavior in myriad personal and professional situations might well be thought of as deeply offensive or highly disrespectful in numerous cultures.

~~~~~

Always be aware your nonverbal language contains messages that can be interpreted in many different ways by different individuals throughout today's world. It's crucial, therefore, as you interact with your domestic and international neighbors, you spend as much time understanding the potential consequences of your body language as you do your verbal skills.

Your attitudes further energize your words that, in turn, energize your actions. In fact, much (if not all) of your body language is rooted in the attitudes you possess. When your attitude is optimistic and respectful towards a specific person, situation, or idea, you are much more inclined to express positive messages and positive actions.

The totality of your nonverbal communication, therefore, has the potency to strengthen and reinforce every message you convey to others. It, oftentimes, can also mean the difference between your listeners quietly receiving your message and one they *enthusiastically* embrace.

~~~~~

No doubt, by paying special attention to cultural values and behavior in several parts of our modern world, you will be a more astute communicator with your words and nonverbal movements. Likewise, with your heightened civility, you will definitely be a Goodwill Ambassador for America as you travel throughout the world.

Chapter 12
Do Your Actions—
and Expectations—
Speak Louder Than Your Words?

It's readily apparent people often measure the worth of other human beings by the actions they demonstrate in their day-to-day behavior. Not surprisingly, then, the same people become very impatient with politicians and other leaders whose daily actions contradict the words and philosophy they espouse in their public comments, television interviews, and speeches. In short order, people will judge you and your integrity on your actions—and how they match your words!

Sounds like a simple observation, doesn't it? Yet, so many people in contemporary America regard their words as just that—words—and seldom ensure their actions match the words they use in conversation. These people then wonder why they lose the trust of colleagues and friends!

If you want to make a positive impact on others in your personal and public life, you must decide what your expectations are for succeeding in life; for being honest with everyone in your life; and for establishing a reputation for consistently following through on any pledge you make to others. Remember, a promise made is a debt unpaid!

As many sociological and psychological studies of human behavior have effectively demonstrated, rising expectations bring rising results. Never is that point made clearer than in the example of using nonverbal communication to support your messages. Once you have *internalized* an attitude—for example, graciousness or pessimism—it is very much evident in all you do as well as in all you say.

Expectations function as potent fueling agents in human communication because they determine the willingness of a person to sustain honest and open communication with others. A genuine and meaningful dialogue always occurs between two people who want to communicate in a sincere and flexible manner.

Moreover, your expectations are the *mental* elements that play significant roles in your nonverbal communication. Such expectations reflect numerous aspects of your personality and your life experiences.

Your expectations are frequently the culmination of:

- Your memories of past experiences and events
- Your hopes and plans for the future
- Your current attitudes, deriving from the beliefs, values, and prejudices you have inherited from a variety of sources, such as your family, friends, education, culture, and physical environment
- Your strong feelings pertaining to contemporary events and your current worldview.

- Your profound interest—or lack thereof—in other people and things
- Your assumptions about various people, places, cultures, ideas, situations, and lifestyles different or unfamiliar to you

Personal expectations are unusually strong personality factors because they have the potential to create in you number of feelings and attitudes. Among these are:

- Positive energy
- Negativism
- Physical and mental awareness
- Frustration
- Nervousness
- Enthusiasm
- Acceptance
- Relaxation
- Optimism

Never forget the emotions resulting from your expectations clearly reflect in your eyes, facial expressions, gestures, and posture. So, what you think has much to do with how well you communicate with people in your family, community, workplace, and all other areas of your life.

~~~~

For years, it has been clear many educators and psychologists, to name two groups of professionals, strongly believe in the theory that *rising expectations bring rising results*. Time after time it has been shown students, patients, employees, and other groups will improve their performance and outcomes in whatever activity they are engaged when their teachers, doctors, managers, and so forth expect them to do so! Naturally, when *anyone* in these groups internalizes that same expectation, the consequences are even more impressive.

It makes sense then we can vastly enhance our communities by expecting more civility from others—and ourselves—in our daily life. First of all, we must remind ourselves all human beings are valuable and deserve basic respect from their families, friends, and even strangers. Secondly, we need to recognize all of us are part of the same human community. Finally, we need to internalize the words President John F. Kennedy forcefully expressed in a televised speech on June 11, 1963 following the admission that day of the first black students to the University of Alabama in Birmingham: "the rights of every man are diminished when the rights of one man are threatened."[25]

It's also wise to adopt another related philosophy about the extraordinary value of each human being that can be described very simply: you are no better than any other person, and no other person is better than you in this world. Powerful words to live by, for certain, but they serve as a strong reminder we *all* belong here in this world, and, with this *right*, we have a *responsibility* to everyone else in this world.

---

[25] Matthews, Chris 2017 *Bobby Kennedy: A Raging Spirit* Simon & Schuster (page 245)

You further reinforce these principles of humility and empathy by constantly increasing and refining the civility you show to others. These include both the people who are familiar to you and those who happen to cross your path for the first time. Only by taking such steps will you ever be sure your attitudes and actions are grounded in a keen sense of integrity, decency, and dignity.

~~~~~

In today's political climate, you quickly learn where people stand by their support or disdain of certain issues and political figures. It speaks volumes about you when *you* align yourself with a president, senator, or congressional representative whose views you endorse. Yet, when this same leader supports policies that benefit you financially (or in some other way) but are policies that undermine your strong principles, you may face an enormous dilemma. Or not.

Though critical issues confronting America today can be viewed from many angles, your decision to assist or stand behind a specific political leader clearly announces to everyone what is most important to you. In other words, there is no way to remain nonpartisan when it involves your political choices. Whom you support and what you support are and will always be your political legacy to our country!

Consequently, it's vital you choose leaders who support your carefully considered viewpoints—viewpoints, of course, that are good for you and good for all of your fellow citizens. Not only will your mind rest easier; you will also avoid a potential crisis of conscience.

Far too often we see our elected leaders and officials enriching themselves with their advocacy for laws, policies, and other political candidates. This destructive behavior does great harm not only to the dignity of their offices; it gravely disheartens their constituents whom they have promised to serve honestly and uncompromisingly.

The current state of politics in our nation absolutely demands that all Americans stop enabling insincere and inept leaders. It's not enough to say merely, "I disagree with his or her point of view" or "I'm disgusted with, and embarrassed by, his or her behavior and actions." We must let these politicians know—with votes, letters, phone calls, and in-person meetings—we don't approve of their actions, and we will not support their immoral or self-serving activities in any manner.

If this strategy seems antagonistic or confrontational to you, then consider this. Many friends and relatives, when dealing with loved ones engaged in self-destructive behavior because of alcohol or drug addiction, finally say, "I am not going to put up with this anymore." Concurrently, the same people decide they no longer will *enable* these individuals in their addiction. These *former* enablers then stop providing money (and other forms of financial assistance), housing, and even emotional support to these addicts so they will begin to take responsibility for the quality of their lives.

Using this strategy as a model in the world of politics, we can and must stop enabling leaders who are more concerned with their own selfish desires and enriching themselves than they are with the genuine needs of their constituents. When you stop enabling poor leadership, whether on a local, state, or national level, you will help build a much more productive, peaceful, and unified society.

Keep in mind, too, the one concept all politicians clearly understand is the power of voting! So, the first, and most obvious, way to stop enabling leaders—your mayor, council members, congressional representative, senator, or president, for example—is by voting for uniquely qualified candidates who will take actions that honestly reflect *your* concerns, goals, beliefs, and values. Never underestimate the power of your one vote. It is one of the biggest change agents at your disposal to improve your community and the greater American society of which you are a vital part!

~~~~~

There are several major forces that prevent increased civility in politics: aggressiveness, negativism, a focus on destroying people's reputations, and a lack of fairness and respect.

The idea of winning at all costs has prevailed for way too long in the USA. In its path, this approach to politics has destroyed people's lives; unfairly rewarded candidates and elected officials who don't play by the rules; and soured many people of all ages, who have tremendous ambition and innovative ideas, from entering politics.

So, what can we do to restore civility to an area of American life that once was respectful and responsive to everyone? The concept of civility implies a graciousness and courtesy to those with whom we interact. Naturally, to demonstrate these qualities, we need to be positive in all of our dealings with others—even those with whom we disagree—in the political arena.

We should not accept negativism or hypocrisy in any area of politics, be it in campaign advertising, political debates, press coverage, primaries, elections, or even in day-to-day discussions of any political issue or politician. Otherwise, we will contribute to a growth of rumors, lies, inuendoes, deceptive propaganda, and personal vendettas in our country's civic behavior. Such conduct clearly undermines and damages our democratic way of life in America—not to mention the influence it has on people to avoid politics altogether.

In our daily conversations and activities, we must also be careful to avoid harming or destroying another person's character or high standing in our communities while promoting our own objectives and agendas. People sometimes thoughtlessly (and dangerously) pass along false or inaccurate data about another person's views, actions, and personal background. And, before long, such damaging information creates almost insurmountable barriers for the person to overcome and gravely hurts (if not ruins) his or her image locally, nationally, or internationally.

In all of our civic life, we must employ fairness and respect if we are to live up to the values and tenets enshrined in our laws, proclamations, and democratic vision. These qualities are not as easy to implement as they may sound when people feel very strongly about a viewpoint or become intensely emotional when describing their reactions to certain situations.

These principles of fairness and respect further require us to stop shouting at people; insulting them with sarcastic remarks; and interrupting or talking over them during a debate or discussion. Nothing really is gained when we treat others in a rude or insensitive way, especially when a person does so only to score political points with a specific audience.

It's wise to remind ourselves the concept of communication implies an awareness of another person (or persons) who is the recipient of any ideas, opinions, suggestions, and convictions we choose to transmit. So, it's crucial we adhere to the highest standards of behavior if we want to engage in healthy and productive communication with others.

Undeniably, empathy must be the basis for any respect and fairness you demonstrate to other people. Try as deeply as you can to place yourself in their situations. Try also to understand their circumstances and their reactions to these circumstances. And, before offering your feedback or response to them, think carefully about what they have expressed to you.

Then look for common ground between the two of you. In other words, find a viewpoint on which you do agree—and say so to your communication partner! This is both a thoughtful and diplomatic way to segue into expressing your own opinions on the same subject.

~~~~~

Patriotism: love and loyal or zealous support of one's country.

Patriot: fellow citizen; a person who loves and loyally or zealously supports his or her own country.

In light of the brouhaha about professional athletes not standing during the national anthem, let's be clear. Patriotism, like religion, is best exemplified by "not wearing it on your sleeve" to paraphrase a familiar maxim. It is far more impressive to witness a person's patriotic *actions* and the benefits they bring to other Americans and visitors to our country.

To be even more direct, let's remember our American flag is a *symbol* of our country; it is not our country. For example, many Christian churches have statues of people elevated to sainthood. But the people who pray in these churches are aware the statues are just symbols—representations, if you will—of a particular person and his or her Christian life. The statues, of course, are not real people nor are they animated in any way. So, people are not normally offended when others don't put a hand over their heart or clasp their hands together in prayer fashion as an act of deference to the statues.

Quite frankly, where is the connection between people standing while singing America's national anthem and their strong loyalty to America? That's like saying, "If people visit their church, temple, or mosque once a week and sing or chant religious music, then they are more religious (and, by implication, morally superior) to other people who don't participate in the music or don't even visit a place of worship on a regular basis."

More to the point, symbolic behavior is not only hollow with its emphasis on immutable behavior and unyielding formality; it is also dangerous because it requires everyone to be the same, do the same, and stay the same. Such unbending conformity is stifling because it suffocates all that is different, creative, spirited, and individualistic in a person, and leaves, in its place, a fervor that breeds only fear, fundamentalism, and, over time, fanaticism.

There are numerous instances in history where this *hollow patriotism* has led to extreme prejudice that, in turn, resulted in violence and cruelty towards large groups of people throughout the world. Just think of what happened in Germany in the 1930-1940s when the Nazi Party and its sympathizers were ruthlessly determined to identify the *true Germans*, the people who were the unquestionable members of the *Aryan* race.

In their zeal—and, often, because of their tremendous fear—neighbors, friends, and family members betrayed others (including their own relatives) who didn't act or look like *true Germans*. Adolph Hitler, the leader of both Germany and the Nazi Party, used rigid conformity to his extraordinarily vile advantage to eliminate anyone who was inferior, apathetic, or hostile to Naziism.

In Hitler's resolve to dominate all of Germany and other parts of Europe, he insisted that all people who genuinely loved Germany must salute the Nazi flag with their right arm extended forward while proclaiming, "Heil Hitler." And woe be to any German citizen, along with any person of a country that Germany had invaded, who did not stand up and salute the Nazi flag while blurting out, "Heil Hitler." In the end, Adolph Hitler and his followers murdered over six million people, many of them gassed to death and burned in ovens; shot to death on a street near their home; or starved to death in horrifying concentration camps.

When any person or leader in our country demands loyalty from our citizens by *insisting,* they stand when our national anthem is sung, we, as Americans, have indeed started to move down the proverbial slippery slope. Sadly, this slippery slope is destined to end only in distress, brutality, and destruction of all that we love and enjoy today in the United States. This artificial patriotism is just one more reason we should never forget the perceptive words of the legendary President Teddy Roosevelt in describing patriotism: *Patriotism means to stand by your country. It does not mean to stand by the president.*

~~~~~

Gazing at the landscape of America today, it's relatively easy to see a country full of citizens divided into two distinct groups: people who want the United States of America to be the nation they perceive it once was and the people who perceive the United States of America as it could be. And this divide grows larger every day because fear is the driving force of one group, and mounting restlessness is the driving force of the other group.

Those who want America as it used to be cling to their earlier versions of a country they once knew, and they fear the many changes that are facing it. The other group believes the America they knew earlier has already been altered by many changes, but they welcome change as a way to make our country better, stronger, and more welcoming to new citizens.

The first group, whom we call traditionalists, apparently fears change and the adjustments it requires in their lives—with perhaps a slight realization that the old ways have become outdated and irrelevant to an America approaching 2020. Meanwhile, the other group, to whom we refer as futurists, embraces change because it offers more opportunities, experiences, and benefits to enrich their lives and the lives of their fellow citizens.

The divide between these two factions in our country continues to grow wider and more immovable because of each group's stubborn position. The traditionalists cling to the past and the way things used to be. So, they are full of anxiety because they fear their way of life will be seriously altered or even eliminated in a few years. They naturally become very resistant when they believe new people, new policies, and new methods of doing things will replace what is familiar and comfortable to them.

The traditionalists have spent their lives expecting no major upheavals in their daily routines. For them, the familiarity and consistency in their lives have given them a sense of safety and security they believed would last throughout their lives.

The futurists, on the other hand, favor an ongoing shift in the ways our country does things. They feel—and have felt for a long time—the United States must continually evolve so their lives will remain happy, healthy, and productive.

For these advocates of adaptation, change is a favorable way to improve the America they know and ensure a better life for both their neighbors and themselves. These citizens strongly believe change is natural, necessary, and nourishing for any country that wants to grow and thrive.

Futurists also regard America as part of a large global network in which international neighbors care for, protect, and help each other to advance in numerous areas. With such cooperation in fields, including education, healthcare, the environment, farming, economics, and technology, these futurists are confident all global citizens will enhance their lives and create a world that leads to peace.

Still, numerous people continue to ask two critical questions. Why is there such obvious anger among different groups in the United States who disagree about politics and other controversial subjects? Why is this anger so intense? Some people would probably respond to both of these questions with a similar answer. The vast emotional distance among these Americans stems from years of frustration with each other's condescension, arrogant behavior, and self-righteousness.

Or others might say many Americans have forgotten their country has always been a cauldron of diverse ideas, opinions, and beliefs. Moreover, they might add, we would not be the unique country we are without this diversity of thought. No doubt, these people readily identify with and understand the wisdom of the United States motto: E plurbus unum (out of many one).

However, an even more urgent question to ask is, "How do we find common ground again and regain respect for the divergent views of those with whom we disagree?" A practical beginning may be reminding ourselves about the philosophical beliefs inherent in the laws and concepts found in the US Constitution and the Declaration of Independence. Also, it wouldn't hurt any of us to read and grasp the fundamentals of the United States government by parsing *every* sentence in these documents. By doing so, we are sure to have a deeper understanding of the intentions (and deliberate omissions) of America's Founding Fathers and the doctrines they espoused.

The American people have strenuously debated many national events and policies related to critical events occurring in the past few years. So, we have a definite responsibility—a duty, really—as American citizens to make sure all of our opinions, ideas, and arguments are based on the truth, aka facts. When it comes to the foundation of our democratic government, there are no fake facts!

We also need to listen, both in public and private settings, to those people whose irritable, petulant attitude and remarks often put us in a defensive state within seconds. Just by listening more closely to these individuals, we may find a small part of their political perspective with which we do agree. If so, we can use that little source of agreement to open a new line of communication with the same people.

As a Democrat, for example, you may concur with your fervent Republican colleague you, too, believe taxes must be cut for various income levels to improve the overall economy. Using that as a starting point, you could further the dialogue by asking the other person about various areas of taxation that could be agreeable to both Republicans and Democrats. Simply by having a civil and lengthy conversation with people with whom you often disagree can increase the mutual respect and understanding between you.

~~~~~

Looking at the conflict of values and divisiveness among Americans today, all of us can potentially name several factors that led us to this unfortunate juncture. Each of us undoubtedly has an opinion as to the way we must restore the civility that once was a distinct feature of American life.

Nonetheless, as an answer to the question that serves as the title of Chapter 12, we need to make our actions and expectations speak louder—much louder and more forcefully—than our words could ever do. Whether we're concerned about improving our schools, community safety, political life, business practices, or outreach to marginalized members of our towns and cities, we must be actively involved as American citizens.

Primarily, we need to put our expectations to work *now* and not have them just remain on our to-do list! So, it's essential for all of us to get involved as soon as possible in the areas of need that matter most to us. We can contribute our time and talents to improve our communities or to make a difference in the lives of less fortunate individuals. The key is to regard any and all of our contributions as urgent and necessary to create a better and kinder America.

Secondly, it's sometimes not enough to just give money to a cause. Many people often say we must be the *change agents* we expect! Therefore, we must also give our ideas, energy, and enthusiasm to the areas affecting the quality of our lives and that of our neighbors. If we don't do so, then we really cannot criticize nor complain about the way things are.

It's amazing what happens when a person offers even only a few hours a week assisting and serving others in a variety of community settings: conducting literacy programs; working in soup kitchens; cataloging books at a library; cleaning up parks and forest preserves; assisting "Neighborhood Watch" committees; teaching citizenship

Do Your Actions—And Expectations—Speak Louder Than Your Words?

classes; taking calls on a suicide hotline; providing basic supplies to homeless people; serving on a church or mosque or temple committee; delivering Meals on Wheels to senior citizens; and on and on and on. What's more amazing is how you—as one person—can make a difference in determining the success of a community program, the future health of a young person or adult, and even whether a person lives or dies.

Many times, we praise people who work on behalf of others and say to ourselves, "I wish I had time to do something so worthwhile." Well, you do, *if* you are willing to readjust your priorities. For example, you could set aside part of a day or evening to volunteer your time, and be part of something that's bigger than you, something that's not about you, and something that becomes even better and stronger *because of you*!

Activism of any sort is bound to serve you and your community well. When you volunteer your time and effort, you are indeed *saving* a lot of money for a program or an organization; you are becoming a fine example of generosity; and you are undoubtedly enriching yourself in a practical, spiritual, and emotional way. Just think what all of those things can do for your psyche alone!

Of course, one of the easiest and most critical ways to be a true activist in your community is to vote in every election that is open to you. You are exercising one of the greatest rights you have as an American citizen whenever you vote in a local, state, and national election. By voting, you are saying loudly and clearly you cherish the right to participate actively in your government's affairs, and you deeply respect the extraordinary sacrifices of all those who came before you and made your right to vote possible.

We frequently talk about the importance of voting to ensure all of our democratic principles and institutions continue to work. Still, there are so many people who choose to stay away from the polls on election day for many reasons. Primary among these reasons is the belief that one person's vote doesn't matter.

As we have seen in several recent elections, the opposite situation is true! One vote can, and often does, make a difference as to a particular person being elected to a specific office; a certain law being passed; or additional funds being granted for a new community facility, such as a school. Furthermore, your one vote can alter legal guidelines affecting all of us; promote infrastructure projects enhancing our neighborhoods and communities; and create policies having a direct impact on our families' economic well-being. It may be a cliché, but *every vote does count* when citizens' needs and dreams are at stake.

Don't ever forget we live in a country that, compared to so many countries throughout the world, gives us unparalleled freedom, security, and access to innumerable resources which help all of us grow as human beings. Ultimately, we have a responsibility to ourselves—and to our fellow citizens—to respect and value our voting rights because these rights frequently are the basis for so much that is available to us as Americans.

Putting it in more colloquial terms, every time you vote you are sending a thank you note to the United States of America. And, in this note, you are expressing your deep appreciation to our nation for all you have and all you are as an American citizen.

Unquestionably, your expectations have an immense effect on your thought processes and actions. You will discover that the enduring link between what you honestly believe and what you eventually do is the foundation of much satisfaction and success in your life.

Chapter 13
Managing Anger to Maintain Civility

Here is a bit of wisdom for you to ponder: profanity is the crutch of a weak mind when it comes to civility in the language we use every day to communicate with others. Yet, it appears numerous people are displaying more and more mental weakness in their day-to-day oral communication.

Whether it's discussing politics, arguing about a personal slight, or describing an unpleasant person or a person with whom they disagree, these men and women apparently think injecting vulgar four-letter words (or other off-color language) adds emphasis and strength to their comments. Still, there are many people who are completely baffled as to how profane or vulgar words enhance *any* oral or written communication.

Sordid language is so commonplace we almost have come to expect it from others. But let's consider for a moment the linguistic quality that obscene words contribute to a conversation or discussion.

For example, a person refers to someone he or she dislikes or disdains as a f***ing a**hole or some other vulgar term. This obscene term merely reflects the speaker's inability to explain accurately the essence or actions of another human being. Most of the time, obscene words utterly fail to describe the speaker's angry reaction to the person's behavior, values, or personality in any literal way. Even in a figurative sense, the same obscene words often do not focus on the speaker's specific complaints about the other person's shortcomings.

> Author's note: Incidentally, we recently checked our dictionary concerning the vulgar term mentioned on the previous page, and, not surprisingly, the term remains descriptive of body functions and body parts.

So, one might wonder about the usefulness of such a vapid description. Stated with a very sarcastic or angry tone of voice, these words, of course, convey the speaker's strong aversion to the person, but utterly fail to issue a vigorous and complete rebuke to a person about his or her *explicit* behavior or attitude.

On the other hand, it would be much more civil for the speaker to avoid profanity and simply state a forceful response to the other person's improper attitude or conduct with statements similar to the following, "I *strongly* believe you shouldn't have done (or said) that, but I forgive you." Or, "I think you were *very* rude to me, but I hope you'll be kinder to the next person." Or "I'm completely surprised you acted that way, but I refuse to yell or scream about what you did because it's not worth wasting my energy."

It's obvious a speaker will endear himself or herself to far more people when using language that is free of vulgarity and profanity. To put it more simply, the language skills we demonstrate every day reveal much about our level of intelligence, polish, and, yes, civility.

What Is Anger?

A feeling of displeasure resulting from an injury, mistreatment, opposition, etc., and usually showing itself in a desire to fight back at the supposed cause of this feeling.

> *Webster's New World College Dictionary*, Fifth College Edition, Copyright 2016 by Houghton Mifflin Harcourt, Inc.

Innumerable people are unaccustomed to expressing their anger appropriately. So, they frequently use angry words and behaviors during any unpleasant confrontation with another person. It's obvious these angry people often react to others without considering their own feelings.

It's necessary to know anger is a normal reaction. However, it is always preceded by another feeling. And that feeling is always caused by an unmet need.

Anger, once again, is:

- Normal
- An unmet need
- Always preceded by another feeling

Before you can resolve angry situations, you must know who the angry person is and why the person is angry. Otherwise, your relationship with this person will remain tense, counterproductive, and volatile where anything can happen—and often does—because you avoid or deny anger in yourself or in your coworkers.

Do you avoid conflicts and arguments because they make you uncomfortable? Would you rather not discuss behaviors that bother you? Or do you feel justified in speaking directly to a person who has bothered, inconvenienced, or hurt you in some way?

How do you feel about angry confrontations? So often, your reaction to anger originates with childhood experiences. Your parents or other caregivers may have taught you that anger is improper, inappropriate, immature, rude, or offensive. These same people may have taught you anger is also a major violation of etiquette. This prohibition of anger often stems from several childhood experiences, notably the observance of the *unwritten rules* of what constitutes polite behavior established by one's family. Even today, a voice from somewhere still tells many people, just when their anger is building, "Nice people don't get angry."

It is important for you to realize anger is a natural part of your emotional makeup as a human being. Anger is also one of your responses to myriad stimuli that may confuse, frighten, or threaten you in either direct or indirect ways. As with all emotions, anger is an emotion that you choose to employ—or choose not to employ—throughout your life. Thus, anger is a possible and *normal* outlet for you as you cope with and try to improve situations in your life.

It is critical to remember, nonetheless, when you become angry, some other feeling happened first. That feeling further creates and develops a life of its own when a particular need or expectation you have remains unfulfilled. In other words, anger is energy set into motion when your needs or expectations are not met.

Then anger begins to manifest itself in your *thoughts*, *feelings*, and *behaviors*. Taken together, these three aspects of anger have tremendous influence on your emotional and physical state. On the other hand, the sequence of events related to your anger changes if any one of the three—thoughts, feelings, or behaviors—changes.

You choose to be angry just as you choose to be happy, loving, and so forth. It is normal for you to experience anger, but what you do with your anger is up to you. *You* become responsible for the consequences of your anger.

You will better understand how and why emotions get in the way of clear communication when you listen attentively to others and observe their behavior carefully. This valuable information will assist you in clarifying and correcting misunderstandings before they become obstacles. In addition, you will be much more in tune with your own emotions so all of your relationships in and out of the workplace are nurturing, productive ones.

When your anger invades the boundaries of others or hurts people in *any* way, then it is being expressed very inappropriately and is out of control. Likewise, if your anger violates anyone's dignity, physical and psychological well-being, or self-esteem, it is very inappropriate and out of control.

At this point, your anger is no longer anger. Rather, it has become rage, fury, or violence. This means your emotional state is not only improper and threatening; *it has reached the crisis stage*.

Our fast-paced, demanding, and confusing lives have all the potential to create tense and emotionally charged situations for us and those around us. As an adult human being, you have a major responsibility to confront your feelings of anger honestly and deal with them effectively.

Anger that is expressed appropriately:
- Builds understanding
- Promotes trust
- Clears the air.

~~~~~

In fact, anger was a normal outlet for the Founding Fathers of America who vehemently argued and disagreed about so many issues in creating a new nation. There was often a great deal of shouting, sarcastic remarks, and disparaging comments hurled between and among the colonists as they struggled to reach a compromise pertaining to the exact wording of a document or the reasoning behind the creation of a new law. Presidents John Adams and Thomas Jefferson, considered intellectual giants both then and now, were just two of many historic figures in America who frequently argued with each other in a vociferous and angry manner.

So, don't discount anger as irrelevant in a heated discussion, argument, or debate. In some ways, your anger—when based on a deep passion for your viewpoint—can be quite motivational for you and your communication partner. In addition, it can help both of you understand a concept, idea, or conviction with greater clarity and trigger new ways to approach or solve a specific problem, challenge, or source of divisiveness.

Nonetheless, you must always keep your anger under control as you would with any other emotion your experience. You should, of course, do whatever it takes to return to a calm state if you sense anyone around you is feeling uneasy or uncomfortable because of your anger.

Managing Your Anger

Can you manage anger in constructive and healthy ways? To show you can, we have provided a number of anger management techniques on the next several pages. These tips will help you reduce or resolve your anger in a practical manner as well as help you interact capably with an angry person. (It should be noted, too, experts on anger management do not universally agree on all of these techniques.) Remember, effective anger management should cater to *your* individual needs and personality.

To guarantee you deal well with your anger—and never reach the crisis stage—you must remember that all of your anger *can* be expressed properly with a wide assortment of beneficial verbal and nonverbal techniques described on pages 234 to 238. Keep in mind these methods for expressing your anger will help you in significant ways. They will relieve tension in your body; give you more mental relaxation; and ensure you focus more clearly on resolving the situation that caused your anger.

Tools for Managing Your Anger

Arts and Creative Expression

Arts and Creative Expression will assist you in identifying who or what is the target of your anger.

- Create a scribble drawing using only colors that describe what your anger looks like.
- Make a collage of feelings related to your anger.
- Draw a picture depicting the event that caused your anger.
- Write a poem, limerick, short essay, or song about your anger.

Journal or Script Writing

Journal or Script Writing will aid you in understanding your anger before you begin to manage it.

- An anger journal is most effective when it is written on a daily basis for seven days.

  Important Reminder: The reward for expressing anger is not always in resolving the problem. It is expressing, in the most appropriate way, how you feel.

  If you expect your efforts to alter a person's behavior or his or her personality, you may be setting yourself up to become even angrier. You cannot change or fix another human being!

- Your anger journal asks five questions:

> What person or event caused you to be angry today?

> Why did this person or event cause you to become angry?

> What did you do about the situation? (Write about your repressed feelings.)

> What reaction did you receive when you expressed your anger? (Or how did you react when you were the recipient of another person's anger?)

> What would have improved the outcome of this situation? (Some possibilities include an apology, an appeal for clarification, a request to change a behavior or attitude, or a discussion of what you believe would resolve the conflict.)

Physical Activities

Physical Activities are useful in sublimating angry energy into cathartic exercise-oriented workouts. Research has proven such physical activities can be beneficial for your physical, emotional, and mental health.

Be careful, however! For people who are extremely angry, some forms of physical activity can lead to more hostile and aggressive behavior toward others. Two examples of such counterproductive activities are football and soccer.

A list of suggested physical activities for *anger workouts* follows:

- Hitting baseballs in a batting cage
- Driving golf balls at a driving range
- Swinging tennis balls against a wall
- Kneading clay or dough
- Striking a punching bag or pillow
- Engaging in primal screaming

Take a Timeout

If a conversation between you and another person becomes heated or uncomfortable, say these words, "I am beginning to feel angry, and I need to take a timeout!" This is a signal for *both* of you to stop discussing the problem for one hour.

You must meet with this person after the hour has passed, and again try to resolve the problem. If tempers flare anew, take another one-hour timeout. If this timeout does not work, try a 24-hour timeout. Both you and the other person, however, must agree to calm down during this 24-hour period.

Relaxation Techniques

Be certain to relax after an angry outburst occurs. These techniques will help you do just that:

- Take a deep breath and hold it for five seconds. Now, slowly exhale. While exhaling, say to yourself, "Relax, relax, relax."

  You can do this instant drill anywhere or anytime. For example, practice it in your car, right after someone cuts you off in traffic, or while you are standing in a lengthy line at a store or at the post office.

- Engage in progressive muscle relaxation (This requires 15 minutes and a quiet room or quiet space.) Start at your head and work your way down to your toes.

  Concentrate on making each muscle tense; then relax that muscle. Do this with *each* muscle in your face, neck, shoulders, arms, hands, back, stomach, buttocks, legs, and feet.
- Play soft and tranquil music in the background.
- Practice biofeedback or yoga exercises.
- Enjoy a peaceful and soothing massage at a health spa or similar venue.

A Sense of Humor

Anger is not a laughing matter. Or is it? Many experts on anger management encourage you to find humor in the situation that caused you to be angry. Scientists, too, state laughter stimulates your brain to produce alertness hormones. These hormones trigger the release of your body's natural painkillers.

A good belly laugh results in increased blood pressure and heart rate as you gasp for air during the process. When you stop laughing, your pulse and blood pressure drop to lower levels, and your muscles relax. Laughter is one of the most powerful tools in changing your reaction to negative events—events that could, otherwise, result in more destructive anger.

If another person is the focus of your anger, look for humor in the situation involving you and the other person.

- Think of something both of you previously found funny or humorous and relate it to your argument in a nonthreatening way. For example, the two of you may have found it humorous that some colleagues praised you for being a very flexible person when both of you know you, in reality, can be very stubborn.

    So, before the angry confrontation escalates, you say to the other person with an impish smile, "Well, because I am known as a very flexible person, I don't want our disagreement to be unpleasant. I want us to find a solution to our problem."

    In a way, this is more than just a technique to encourage humor. It is also a demonstration of your humility and willingness to restore harmony in your relationship with the person.

~~~~

Bullying—The Antithesis of Civility

We have spent many years discussing the origins and negative effects of bullying behavior that children and teenagers experience in and out of school. However, only recently have people started paying much more attention to adult bullying behaviors and their malignant consequences for others.

Bullying behavior in the adult world is just as insidious, in some ways, as it is for many children and teenagers. Often, there are too few advocates on which to rely in a crisis of adult bullying. In numerous adult settings—business, law enforcement, medicine, and politics to cite a handful of professional areas—we see or feel the effects of the machinations of bullies on display.

Yet, the adult bullies continue to grow and thrive while innumerable people around them—coworkers, prisoners, colleagues, patients, ex-classmates, relatives, friends, and everyday citizens—suffer miserably in silence from the pain inflicted on them, in both overt and covert ways, by such tormentors. As with a legion of children, these adults often don't know where to turn or whom to trust in relating their stories of being bullied (mentally, emotionally, physically or all three). This is particularly evident when the tormentor is in a position of power or has access to others with greater authority.

Plus, there is a large segment of our population who were raised with the idea if you can't say something positive or kind about someone else, you should remain silent That may sound like good advice to people who don't want to get involved or who are afraid of aggressive individuals, but it's terrible advice for American citizens who want to have the courage to confront violent and ignorant people; to create a safe environment for themselves and those around them; and to think ethically, solve problems, and focus on the future. Quite simply, remaining silent in the face of calamity is, most times, not an option for these people.

Yes, you might be putting yourself in a dangerous position when dealing with a bully either directly or indirectly. Speaking directly to the bully or indirectly to the bully (by asking others to address the bully on your behalf) could both lead to further repercussions. It's possible either option could cause unseen problems because bullies are often unpredictable. But do you want to live up to your principles at all costs to stop the bully from inflicting more harm on you and others? Or are you comfortable as long as you can pacify the bully so he or she doesn't bother *you*? These are tough questions certainly, but only you can answer them.

Nonetheless, you do have other sources of relief to consider, each dependent on the level of bullying that exists. You can enlist more people to join you in defying a bully because there is always strength in numbers. You can also contact people in authority, with excellent reputations for solving bullying problems, to assist you in contacting the appropriate police departments and other law enforcement agencies. In addition, you can ask people who know the bully well (and who are also friendly or close to you) to intercede for you with the understanding you are not trying to intimidate or malign the bully. You simply are requesting a relationship with him or her that is more peaceful, productive, and comfortable.

Bullying in any sphere of life is a profoundly disturbing behavior problem that cannot be easily solved. But it does help you to acknowledge it is a menacing and counterproductive behavior that continues to grow—unless there is an impediment placed to prevent its buildup or elimination. This applies to bullying in a school, playground, workplace, neighborhood, social event, political arena, or any other environment.

While you consider your options for standing up to bullying behavior, it would be wise for you to ponder these heartfelt thoughts from Reverend Martin Niemöller who survived several years (1937-1945) as a prisoner in the Nazi concentration camps during World War II:

> *First they came for the socialists, and I did not speak out—because I was not a socialist*
>
> *Then they came for the trade unionists, and I did not speak out—because I was not a trade unionist.*
>
> *Then they came for the Jews, and I did not speak out—because I was not a Jew.*
>
> *Then they came for me—and there was no one left to speak for me.*
>
> —Reverend Martin Niemöller

Reverend Niemöller was a German theologian and prominent Lutheran pastor in Germany who was an outspoken critic of Adolf Hitler, leader of Germany's Nazi Party.

Make no mistake! This arrogant, brash, and unseemly behavior has infiltrated Washington, DC! Even at the uppermost levels of our government, we witness bullying on an almost weekly, if not daily, basis. News reports keep us aware of the dubious (and, occasionally, illegal) ways that leaders from the President to Congress to various Cabinet posts and federal agencies are perpetrators of bullying. We often hear and read about high-level officials who threaten and intimidate subordinates to follow their edicts all the while knowing such actions violate the laws of the United States Constitution.[26] Clearly, the dangerous effects of bullying are not limited to some mean girls in high school or a few egotistical fraternity brothers on college campuses.

When bullying of this sort reaches the top echelons of our democratic government, it is not only a major worry for all citizens. It is also apparent all of our citizens must directly confront the problem of adult bullying.

We must demand, through public protests, voting practices, and ongoing collaboration with our elected leaders, that openness and honesty exist in every part of our government! We must also demand a free press so we, as citizens, receive continuous information about our government's goals, activities, and communication with other countries. To do otherwise is to allow America to be terrorized and frightened by those elected to keep us informed, safe, and secure—and not to bully their way to satisfying their own needs and desires.

Handling Angry Confrontations with Other People

You also need to analyze and interpret the angry feelings you receive from others. Again, it cannot be overstated that when someone is angry another feeling preceded the anger.

---

[26] Kindy, Kimberly and Lee, Michelle Ye Hee, 2018, "How a congressional harassment claim led to a secret $220,000 payment" Washington Post, January 14

Finding yourself face to face with an enraged relative, friend, neighbor, or colleague is never a pleasant encounter. Aside from being unpleasant, it can play havoc with your reputation!

The only effective way to settle an argument with another person is to stop arguing as soon as possible and develop a rational solution to your disagreement. This is never easy to do, and it's often quite difficult to do. Situations involving anger are always uncomfortable.

When you are engaged in an angry confrontation, you react in one of three ways: by fighting back, running away, or becoming immobilized. As you ponder these responses to anger, you will recognize they are evolutionary in nature or traced to animalistic instincts. Such responses are our basic instructions for handling instincts and emotions that extend all the way back to the beginning of human evolution.

However, your daily life need not be battleground! As soon as you identify any signs of anger in someone, it's time to make an effort to reduce the pressure and anxiety level.

~~~

The following checklist contains numerous suggestions for dealing with a potentially angry encounter with another person:

- Be aware of the other person's anger.
- Aggressive behavior is often shown by people who
    - Shout

Managing Your Anger to Maintain Civility

- o Shake their fists
- o Glare at others.

➤ Passive-aggressive behavior is often demonstrated by those who

- o Speak sarcastically
- o Withdraw from conversations
- o Blame others.

➤ Check for short, curt sentences spoken by the angry person.

➤ Watch for invasion of your personal space by the other person.

➤ Search for statements of denial (such as, "Nothing's wrong" or "I'm not mad") by the person who is angry.

➤ Look for nonverbal clues (a change of color in the face or neck, for example) of the other person that indicate he or she is angry or extremely anxious about the current situation.

➤ Observe your heart rate. If your heart rate is increasing, the less clearly you can think and communicate your thoughts. If your heart rate (pulse) is greater than 100 beats per minute, BEWARE of potential health danger.

➤ Hold onto your initial response because an angry person may interpret it as a personal attack.

➤ Ask for a timeout. This pause will have a calming effect on you *and* the angry person so both of you can work successfully on a solution.

- Set firm boundaries. Tell the angry person it is not okay with you to be derided, verbally attacked, or interrupted. **Never tolerate inappropriate behavior.**

- Abstain from explaining or interrupting the angry person with your point of view. Doing either of these is a disguise for fighting back.

- Avoid blaming the other person. Blaming is just another form of running away.

- Listen actively to the person who is angry. This tells the person you are paying attention and want to understand his or her viewpoint.

You may find these responses amazingly effective when interacting with an angry individual:

> *"That's quite a problem."*
>
> *"That would concern me, too."*
>
> *"I understand you completely."*
>
> *"I am listening to you."*
>
> *"Please tell me more. I want to know why this bothers you so much."*

- Validate the feelings of the other person. For example, you can employ statements, such as the following ones that reflect validation.

  > *"I can see how upset you are."*
  >
  > *"This clearly involves me, too."*

- Restate the problem. This will help you focus more fully on the immediate predicament. Consider these examples:

    "So, what you're saying is you are annoyed with me because I haven't spoken to two of your coworkers about their tardiness when, in fact, I commented on your tardiness last month."

    "In essence, you're angry because you believe I should not have accepted all the credit for a well-received report that was completed before the deadline."

    Also, you might ask the other party this question:

    "What would you like me to do?"

    NOTE: Be careful to put the emphasis on the words *like* and *do* and not on *me*. This question will help the other person to stop reacting and think more rationally.

- State what *you* want as the solution. All of the following statements are examples of viable solutions.

    "I want both of us to go away winners."

    "I would like to pay you...."

    "I want to arrive at an agreement that is workable and satisfying for both of us."

"I would like you to leave this room feeling you are very valuable to our organization."

"I truly wish for you to believe you are deeply loved by everyone in our extended family."

- Negotiate your terms with the angry person.

    "As I understand it, you want _____, and I want _____, so I'm willing to offer you _____ if you give _____."

    Note: Keep countering until you reach an agreement.

- Ensure verbal acknowledgment of what you both have agreed to do.

    "So, we've agreed that. . .."

    "It's understood that. . .."

    "I will give you _____ if you _____."

- Set a date for a follow-up meeting. In the meantime, both of you will have an opportunity to try out the solution and, if necessary, modify it together.

- Allow the other person to have the last word. Resisting that parting shot is a victory! Don't forget, a victor is not the person who yells the loudest; he or she is the one who remains the calmest.

Lingering Anger in America

The 2016 presidential race, more than any event in recent American history, showed the damaging effects of collective, long-lasting anger in this country. It also clearly demonstrated anger left unchecked or unaddressed can leave people feeling misunderstood, invalidated, or even ignored by many candidates who weren't truly listening to them.

One of the valuable lessons many Americans learned during the last presidential race is the appeal of candidates who recognize and affirm the feelings of the American voters. Furthermore, the 2016 race for the presidency strongly indicated, no matter how outstanding or poor the qualifications of candidates are, the people who were most popular were those who clearly and accurately addressed the values, attitudes, and emotions of millions of Americans. These were the candidates with a firm understanding of contemporary Americans and their expectations for leadership that is bold, unusual, courageous, lively, and authentic.

The 2016 race for the presidency taught Americans another insightful lesson. Candidates greatly appeal to throngs of people who feel forgotten or neglected by their government and its policies—and even perhaps by their own communities. And, in 2016, these people were a very visible and vocal audience on the campaign trail.

In fact, these disgruntled and, often, desperate citizens were *still* angry about losing their jobs, investments, homes, and security during the decade prior to the 2016 election. Their anger had rapidly led to a major distrust of government and their elected officials; a deep belief their way of life was being eradicated and replaced by strange and unfamiliar entities; and an adamant demand that they and their concerns be acknowledged by their government. Moreover, these angry citizens were offended by what they perceived as a blatant disrespect and disregard for their personal opinions and circumstances by many of their political leaders and fellow Americans.

In such an unsettling environment, a forceful candidate, who said in a loud, boisterous, and, often, crass way that he empathized with them and shared their anger, was bound to connect with these angry American citizens. And he *did* because he simply reiterated to them what they had been complaining about for several years!

Furthermore, it was easy for this candidate to do so because he knew angry people—extremely angry people—want others to understand their views and not placate them with platitudes and empty promises. This candidate knew, too, these citizens weren't ready or willing to listen to viable solutions to their problems. They only wanted their candidates to listen to them and validate their candid feelings and opinions *before* offering any of *their ideas*.

Similar to other angry people, these citizens didn't want to be told to calm down; think with a clear head; and work with others on long-term resolutions of their particular difficulties. These people, collectively, were a classic example of an angry person who, because of his ongoing resentment and discontent, has reached the crisis stage!

And, just like any angry individual reaching the crisis stage during a heated argument, these very angry individuals *demanded* two things: to have others agree with their complaints and to be assured that something would be done immediately to address their problems. So, the previously mentioned candidate easily acquired a legion of fervent followers because he continually ranted about dangers to their health and safety; blamed other people (including several political leaders) for their economic difficulties; and promised them he alone would improve their lives in a very short time.

Not surprisingly, this candidate exploited the fears, insecurities, and, most obviously, the anger of his followers. But there will be a big price to pay for a long time for whatever was gained in the last presidential campaign. The lingering anger and anxiety still being exhibited by millions of Americans only highlight the critical need for all citizens to make decisions on a more inclusive, equitable, and compassionate basis.

In retrospect, the results of the 2016 presidential election may serve as a cautionary tale for all people. Anger, left unchecked, in one person or in millions of people can create enormous communication barriers that are exceedingly hard to remove. These barriers, in turn, can lead to tremendous feelings of distance, disagreement, and doubt between a huge number of citizens and their respective leaders.

For a moment, just think of two friends or two relatives, both citizens of the United States, who have a falling-out because they don't agree on a certain political, religious, immigration, or sexuality matter. In addition, they refuse to reach a compromise or, at the very least, "agree to disagree" about their particular views. This quarrel could, unfortunately, last days, weeks, or even years depending on the individual personalities involved. Now, multiply the disagreement between these two people that lasts for years by millions of citizens within America, and the enduring animosity could have disastrous consequences for our country in the future.

As was mentioned earlier in this book, anger *can be* a motivational agent in helping individuals and small groups of people achieve goals as well as discover fresh solutions to problems. When a large population of one nation has reached a critical stage of anger, however, it is imperative that people take a collective timeout to reflect on their views and the reasons they hold these views.

It is essential that angry citizens consider, too, the political beliefs and opinions on which they are willing to compromise with others. Even when discussing some strongly held opinions with flexibility and openness, people are very likely to remove obstacles and initiate new lines of communication with their discussion partners. Of course, all of this effort must be directed towards reaching a compromise among groups holding distinctively different views to ensure long-lasting peace for our nation.

Again, consider the hot button issues facing our Founding Fathers over 240 years ago. There was vehement, and, often, unpleasant resistance between groups about states' rights, property rights, religious freedom, military defense, the levying of taxes, and numerous other controversial subjects. Yet, these men found enough common ground to build a powerful foundation for one of the most extraordinary democracies in world history.

Despite the unsettling events and divisiveness in America in the past few years, we have thankfully not lost the fortitude and focus of our early leaders. So, we can find agreement with others once we make a commitment to communicate honestly as well as to compromise with others on all issues affecting the common good of every American.

It is clear anger, like any other emotion, must be controlled. Otherwise, its unbridled growth negatively affects everything in its path. In many ways, uncontrolled anger, such as we've seen and felt in the United States recently, severely limits our citizens' objectivity and reason. This anger also becomes a monumental barrier in unifying a nation to move forward with work that benefits all citizens, whatever their political views might be.

Most of all, we need to put an end to the out-of-control anger that exists in so many areas of the United States. That means we need to stop shouting at one another; blaming others; insulting those who disagree with us; and deciding our solutions to problems are the only viable ones. The immense energy we're using to express our hostility and impatience with our fellow citizens needs to be channeled into an energy that allows for meaningful discussions; sincere consideration of others' views; and a renewal of cooperation that places our finest principles above our political allegiances.

However, we Americans can restore greater civility throughout our country if we again focus on the common good—and *not* on the good of our party's election results; nor the size of our bank accounts; nor the status we possess in our social circle; nor a presumption of a comfortable and lifetime career in government; nor a close relationship with people in high positions as a means to personal gain. If we can truly shed our anger, and do what we must to protect everyone, especially those still in need in this vast and incredibly wealthy nation, we will be the dynamic, generous, and reasonable nation we have long claimed to be.

All the while, we must keep demonstrating our commitment to a gentle civility that makes all Americans assured they are recognized, appreciated, and rewarded for the unique parts they play in our ever-evolving American life. For, in the end, we will be a truly civilized nation only when *all* of our citizens reap the benefits of compassion, respect, fairness, and peace.

Chapter 14
Frequently Asked Questions and Challenging Situations in Face to Face Communication

In so many settings, people struggle to respond assertively, honestly, or diplomatically (and sometimes, in all three ways) to their communication partners. This chapter, therefore, gives you an array of tough questions and situations you will occasionally face in your daily communication. They summarize the concerns and discomfort people often have about their conversations with others.

You will also learn how to respond suitably and effectively to both the demanding questions and situations mentioned earlier. You will discover, too, it is easy to adapt any of these suggested responses to fit your own particular communication challenges.

Our advice for different conversation dilemmas, meanwhile, contains many ideas and techniques found throughout *Making Civility Great Again*. By applying variations of these strategies, you will clearly improve your speaking, listening, and nonverbal skills. In the process, you will enhance your civility with everyone you meet.

Just keep in mind feelings are what make us human. All of your feelings are normal and reflective of human nature. But *you choose* to act on your feelings. Equally important, it is *you* who can learn healthy ways to express your feelings.

Frequently Asked Questions About Face to Face Communication

How can I respond effectively to end a conversation about politics with someone who clearly has no inclination to change his or her views?

Well, I can see we both have definite views about politics. And I appreciate you taking the time to offer your opinions because I've learned a great deal from our conversation.

Now, it appears both of us have a better understanding of how other people approach politics in a way that is different from our own.

~~~~~

Let's assume you're discussing a political issue with others at a dinner party in another person's home, and someone asks, "Can we not talk about politics now?" (Suddenly, there is silence in the room.) How do you respond appropriately to this person? Incidentally, the host has been participating in the discussion.

Wow! I guess I'm surprised at your reaction. I didn't know discussing politics bothered you. So, let me say, "I'm sorry" if we upset you. But I would also like to know why such a conversation upsets you. In light of all the divisiveness in our country nowadays, I think it's actually healthy for all of us to share our views calmly with others to improve our understanding of their beliefs and attitudes.

~~~~~

What is the best way to reply to a person whose attitude towards a particular issue is different than yours, and the person is starting to raise the volume of his or her voice?

I understand that, like me, you feel very strongly about the issue we're discussing. However, I think we both could use a break from our conversation right now. This will give each of us time to relax and reflect on the points we've already covered. Why don't we resume our conversation tomorrow (or in two hours or next time we meet)?

~~~~~

How do you respond to a person who uses inflammatory language or ethnic slurs (such as "those people," "you people," "your kind," "Massachusetts liberals," "Coastal Elites like you," "towelheads," "Japs," fairies," "jungle bunnies," "chinks," and so forth) during a conversation with you? Also, how do you make it clear to

the person you find his or her language offensive and demeaning?

You've made some interesting comments, but I want to be honest with you, I listen more respectfully and accurately when my communication partner avoids using what I consider labels or offensive language, like "those people," "fairies," or "chinks."

So, I hope we can continue our discussion at a later time without using terms that are offensive and demeaning to each other or to particular groups of people.

~~~~~

How can you end what you perceive is evolving into a nonproductive discussion with another person?

Thank you for spending some time with me though it is apparent to me we have vastly different views and temperaments.

Nevertheless, I'm glad we had this opportunity to exchange our perspectives because I learned a great deal from our brief conversation. Take care, and maybe our paths will cross again.

~~~~~

What is the most effective way to express your positive comments about a political leader (religious leader, major lobbyist, civil rights or sexual rights advocate, spokesperson for a national nonprofit organization, and so forth) when you already know your communication partner doesn't have a high regard for this person?

Though I realize you don't have a high regard for (XYZ person), I hope you will allow me an opportunity to cite the reasons why I admire this person and why I am convinced he (or she) can improve the lives of all Americans in these unsettling times.

~~~~~

What is the best way to communicate with a sibling who, for a long time, has talked with you on a very superficial level? This sibling never asks your personal opinions related to politics, religion, or sexual conduct because he or she believes (and rightfully so) you hold quite different views about these topics.

Nonetheless, this sibling only converses with you about mundane matters to avoid any potential disagreement or unpleasantness. After any conversation with this sibling, you always feel your formerly close relationship has become shallow and less meaningful than it used to be.

Though I may not say it enough to you, I'm really happy we talk often because you mean a lot to me. But, for quite a while, I think our conversations have been superficial because we only talk about things like the weather, our various work and home projects, and updates about our other siblings and relatives.

We never discuss issues like politics, religion, or even sexual-related topics about which, I'm sure, each of us has strong opinions. I'm wondering if you avoid these discussions because you think they will lead to a disagreement and hurt feelings or you're just uncomfortable talking about these subjects in general.

So, I am eager to know your reaction to what I've just said because I very much want to have a more open and honest relationship with you.

~~~~~

How can you tactfully convey your thoughts to another person, whose political views are very different from yours, that you can and do support a president (or any other elected official) who advocates policies you endorse—even though you don't approve of the individual's personal behavior or like his or her personality?

Please understand I am much more concerned with a candidate's official policies than I am with his or her personal behavior.

I may not approve of the person's behavior or even like his or her personality. But I will support that person's candidacy if he or she espouses views and politics with which I agree and think will benefit America. After all, I don't treat politics as a popularity contest.

~~~~~

How do you remain calm while responding diplomatically, yet assertively, to a communication partner who, —during a political discussion, makes arrogant statements, including "You're wrong," "You obviously don't know the facts," and "Don't be ridiculous!"

Also, how should you reply to the same person who displays condescension towards you by smirking, rolling his or her eyes, or using other nonverbal language to express disdain for your views and ideas?

I know we have views that are dissimilar, but I still would like to understand the reasons for your firm beliefs.

On the other hand, I feel disrespected and insulted when you say, "You're wrong," "You obviously don't know the facts," or "Don't be ridiculous." So, I would like you to remember I put much thought and research into the statements and opinions I express.

I also would feel more validated during our discussions if you would use more positive body language instead of smirking, rolling your eyes, and other nonverbal communication that discount me and my message.

~~~~~

You are having a discussion with another person. And you strongly agree with the person's compassionate attitude towards marginalized people and her negative opinions of extremely conservative Republicans who treat such people dismissively. On the other hand, you

definitely find yourself uncomfortable with her contempt for being civil with any rigid Republican.

Keep in mind this person is firmly convinced that civility is not at all effective in confronting extremely conservative Republicans who demonstrate animus, arrogance, and hypocrisy towards all marginalized people.

What is the most effective and honest way to respond to this person?

Let me first state I very much agree with you about the way extremely conservative Republicans treat marginalized people. And I absolutely loathe the obvious animus, arrogance, and hypocrisy shown by extremely conservative Republicans toward marginalized people.

However, I still feel I must treat these Republicans—despite their rigid views—and all people with civility if I am ever to convince them to adopt my beliefs. You might say I believe in applying the civil and nonviolent approach Dr. Martin Luther King used decades ago during the civil rights protests.

Challenging Situations Often Found in Face to Face Communication

He's an embarrassment as our president. So inflammatory and crass.... It's obvious he has an extraordinarily limited knowledge of the US Constitution. I think he's about the worst president America has ever had!

That's quite an accusation! I really am interested in knowing the particular characteristics you have in mind when you refer to our current president as the worst chief executive officer we've ever had. Also, in what way does he reflect extraordinarily limited knowledge of the US Constitution? I'm eager to listen to your responses because so many people have expressed distinct views about our current president.

~~~~~

I don't trust her. She thinks she has all the answers—she and her liberal leaning friends. They just want to run the country their own way and relax the rules on everything.

First of all, how do you define "liberal"? Second, what do you mean when you say these people "want to run the country their own way and relax the rules on everything"? I think it's important to cite precise information when you describe the intentions and behavior of a group of politicians and their associates.

~~~~~

Oh! Another gun rights nut case! He (or she), no doubt, is in favor of concealed weapons for all gun owners and believes assault weapons are okay for people to store in their homes.

This is a very volatile issue on which to pass judgement on others. So, I would appreciate knowing what evidence you have for thinking this person favors concealed weapons for all gun owners. Also, what proof do you have that this individual believes it's okay for people to store assault weapons in their homes? I'm sure you can see how erroneous information about a person's opinion pertaining to weapons of any kind can be very damaging to him or her.

~~~~~

When will these evangelicals stop trying to inject Jesus into every part of government? I swear some of these people would like to get rid of anyone who is an atheist or an agnostic. I am so tired of hearing what they deem immoral—like gay relationships, abortion rights, and people who don't attend church services. I'd like to say to all of them, in response to what they regard as immoral, "How do these people's actions hurt you?"

Let's be realistic about people involved in the Evangelical movement. They do have a right to talk about Jesus and relate this topic to every part of their life.

But I agree with you on one point. Some evangelicals do embrace all the views you mention. Still, I think it is dangerous for any of us to label an entire group based on the unyielding views held by a minority of people in that group.

I think your last point, meanwhile, is the one we need to focus on the most. When people's actions start to hurt you or anyone else, then, of course, their actions are definitely inappropriate and immoral and may be illegal. So, I strongly believe that's where we need to place our attention—on those people whose actions directly hurt us or other people.

~~~~~

I'm a veteran and I fought for the freedom we have in America. That's why I don't like all these Commies questioning what our President and Congressional leaders say! As far as I'm concerned, they have my back because they are putting our money where it counts—more weapons, more boots on the ground, and more prisons for these drug addicts who are trying to ruin this country.

I certainly can understand your intense feelings about supporting our government. Though I'm not a veteran, I'd like to believe all of us, whether we are veterans or not, have fought in one way or another to preserve the freedoms of every citizen in the United States of America so the person can express his or her opinions without fear of reprisal.

~~~~~

And don't get me started about today's politicians! All they care about is keeping their cushy jobs and not making waves. We used to have politicians who spoke out in defense of certain principles even if their opinions upset their colleagues. Now, what we have is a good old boy network that doesn't care about anything but taking care of its members and their cronies!

I can easily see your point about politicians in the past who spoke out passionately in defense of their principles. It is obvious they put their convictions before their political affiliation.

I agree with you, too, that some current political figures, by their behavior, are demonstrating more concern about themselves and their careers. However, we must not lose sight of the fact there are still some politicians who are truly acting on behalf of the good of our nation.

~~~~~

The problem, as I see it, is the number of people in the USA who want to live off the government with their EBT [Electronic Benefits Transfer] cards, welfare checks, and Section 8 vouchers. These same people don't believe in bettering themselves with education nor do they want to work. It's clear they know how to game the system!

I'm sure, if you were to research all of the safety net programs in the US government, you would discover the money spent on these programs is, in reality, a small percentage of the national budget.

I've actually conducted some research in this area, and I would be glad to share with you the relevant figures I have uncovered. Nonetheless, I assure you, the figures don't indicate a majority of people on welfare are, as you say, "gaming the system."

~~~~~

Why is it, every time I drive through this part of the city, I see more and more foreign names on stores—names I can't even pronounce—and more and more African-American/Asian/Hispanic people? Where are all these people coming from? No wonder we need a wall built to protect America!

Well, if you don't mind, I'd like to mention a couple of facts that might help you understand the many changes now occurring in America. Statistically, a majority of the people in America today are nonwhite, and many of their ancestors were born in non-European nations.

So, unlike four or five decades ago, when many of us older Americans were familiar with names because they were European-derived, we now need to put a little more effort in learning the pronunciation of names. I'm sure you can understand why I am confused as to how a difficult pronunciation of a store name has led you to think we need to build a border wall.

I also think a foreign language dictionary would help all of us lifelong Americans quickly learn many unfamiliar words that are difficult for us to pronounce.

~~~~~

I don't know about these college students. All they seem to do is whine about the triggers that upset them whether it's a campus speaker whose views are different from theirs or a professor who uses speech that isn't politically correct.

Yes. I have wondered about this particular topic myself because there seems to be a lot of focus today on college students and what upsets them.

Still, I think we need to look at the bigger picture. There are tens of thousands of students in the United States who are profoundly serious about their studies and are equally eager to listen to others whose views don't necessarily correlate with theirs or with those of their families.

I believe it is extremely important for all of us to remind college students, who complain about their triggers, that freedom of speech, according to the United States Constitution, allows people in this country to speak on any topic as long as it doesn't incite violence or hate.

~~~~~

If you ask me, anybody found using or selling drugs near a school should be sent to prison for a long time! And that person should not be allowed to live within a half-mile of any school when he or she gets out of prison!

Boy! That's a pretty broad statement. I'm not certain what you're suggesting blends with the idea that, in the United States, the punishment should fit the crime. If a person has been imprisoned because he or she possessed or sold an ounce of marijuana, why would he or she, after leaving prison and living within a half-mile of a school, be a danger to anyone?

In the meantime, I definitely think all of us should spend more of our efforts protecting our children from people who have a history of mental illness and have access to assault weapons.

~~~~~

The way I see it, we should elect judges everywhere in the United States. If judges were elected, you wouldn't have the screwed-up judicial system that's in place today. Too many judges are soft on criminals, especially drug addicts.

You are clearly entitled to your opinion, but I'd like to share my views with you about US judges. I sincerely don't think the whole judicial system is "screwed-up" as you say.

In fact, I'm convinced all of us would be better off if we highlighted the excellent work being done by empathetic and forward-thinking judges in various parts of the United States. These men and women are working hard to reform the judicial system so everyone, including drug addicts, are treated both firmly and fairly.

I also understand many judges are diverting drug addicts to rehabilitation and recovery centers rather than prison. Frankly, I think that strategy is a far more sane, sensible, compassionate, and cost-effective way for dealing with drug addicts who end up in our courts. This approach, too, could help us find better ways to rehabilitate other criminals.

~~~~~

Would someone please explain to me why it's wrong for a wife to stay home to raise her kids, bake cookies, and be the best wife she can be to her husband or wife? In my day, we did that, and it obviously worked, didn't it?

Your plan for women may have worked well several years ago, but I think a woman today should make her own choices in life with the help of her husband or wife. I would also hope the couple would have discussions about the wife's career choices, and those of her spouse, long before they even marry.

I believe times have changed in an economic sense. Many families now count on two incomes just to maintain a reasonable lifestyle.

~~~~~

Why are so many people obsessed with the indiscretions of a president or any other elected official? Let's face it! Many people, who are not in the limelight, do the same things and get away with them. Besides, don't we

have bigger fish to fry considering the problems facing our country?

Indiscretions? Please correct me if I'm wrong, but you seem to be saying it's not a problem if someone gropes a man or woman—or sexually assaults a person—and doesn't get caught. I definitely don't want people to get away with inappropriate, immoral, or illegal behavior, no matter who they are.

As citizens of a democracy, we all have a responsibility to ourselves and to each other. Furthermore, there isn't any room in a democratic society, such as the United States, for people who intimidate or coerce others into any sexual activity or any behavior for that matter!

~~~~~

Oh sure! It's okay to let someone retain his or her driving license—even after being arrested for driving drunk five times in seven years, but someone else, whose kid briefly wanders off from a picnic, has the Department of Children Services threatening to take the child away from him or her because of negligence. Where is the justice in that?

I clearly share your exasperation with the way the justice system sometimes works. Also, for the record, I am convinced a person who has been arrested for driving while intoxicated five times should definitely lose his or her license to drive forever!

I also think many people overreact when a parent slips up and a child wanders off but is found quickly and hasn't been harmed in any way. If all minor mistakes like this were prosecuted, we'd be filling our jails with parents who made small mistakes.

What we need is to make our views known to those who oversee the justice system so all judges are realistic, fair, and empathetic when making their court decisions. Additionally, I believe a brief act of negligence is hardly a major crime.

~~~~~

Once again, it is evident the level of your civility is in direct proportion to how well you listen to others and how well you display your empathy and compassion towards people. Civility, moreover, demands you be receptive to new people, new behaviors, and new ideas so you can grow as an individual while the United States and the world change around you.

As an American citizen, your renewed civility will help restore greater sensibility and sanity to our country as it continues to be a beacon of peace and justice for all people. Most of all, your heightened civility will provide immediate comfort and hope for all those around you who simply seek to be recognized, understood, and respected.

Chapter 15
The Mark of a Truly Civil Person

To create a more robust and harmonious country and to improve our standing in the world, we must insist on greater civility in our day-to-day living. We need to reinforce the courtesy and thoughtfulness, once emblematic of America, whether we are at home, in school, at work, in a store or restaurant, at a sports competition, or in any personal or public setting.

It isn't enough to say, "I'm friendly and I'm polite to others so I do my part to be civil." Civility in contemporary America requires you to be far more sympathetic, empathetic, and generous in spirit to others in your daily activities wherever you are and with whomever you interact—and regardless of how little time you have!

And extending your warmth and kindness to others doesn't cost you any money! Yet, these are extraordinary and valuable gifts to people who receive them from you.

Encouraging someone who is in a hurry to move ahead of you in a line at a coffee shop; allowing a person to pull in front of you in busy traffic; or engaging in a brief, pleasant conversation with a store clerk will certainly provide a refreshing boost to that person—and it will make you feel good, too!

During your day, you may cross paths with homeless people or other individuals who are down on their luck and asking for some money from you so they can eat a meal. Instead of instinctively reacting with the thought, "They should get a job," or "They probably have more money than I do right now," why not let your empathy gene take over and give these people the benefit of your doubt? Maybe they really need money. Or maybe they truly have no access to anyone who can help them. Or maybe they just need a temporary handout and soon will be self-sufficient.

When you tap into your empathy gene, you are often reminded these people are human beings who have many of the same needs, wants, desires, and dreams as you do. And, like you, they may have lived most of their lives in more comfortable surroundings and may have had a family who loved, nurtured, and protected them.

Or maybe they *weren't* blessed with the same opportunities and advantages that were given to you. Nonetheless, because of their education, life experiences, and exposure to different circumstances (both very uplifting and exceedingly difficult), they may well share or understand many of the values you already cherish.

So, for just a few moments, maybe you can imagine yourself in the same situation as these men and women. aybe, you can offer them, if not money or food or anything tangible, your *time* and a sincere greeting that makes them feel like they belong, like they are important, and, most meaningful of all, like they are human beings! When you react like this to others, you are not only being compassionate; you are also demonstrating civility that is genuinely kind, honorable, and authentic.

About the Authors

Kim Kerrigan

Kim Kerrigan has spent most of his adult life as an educator and corporate trainer throughout the United States and Mexico. He is also the editor of a personal memoir, *Mom in Her Own Words*, and is a popular workshop presenter and guest speaker. Mr. Kerrigan cofounded Corporate Classrooms and resides in the Boston area.

Steven Wells

Steven Wells has had a diversified career: engineering executive, information technology entrepreneur, and marketing professional. He currently serves as marketing and content development director for Corporate Classrooms of which he is a cofounder. Mr. Wells lives in the Boston area.

CPSIA information can be obtained
at www.ICGtesting.com
Printed in the USA
BVHW041829080419
544942BV00019B/256/P